BLUEPRINTS

Mental Arithmetic
Key Stage 1

Liz Hopkins

Stanley Thornes (Publishers) Ltd

Stanley Thornes for TEACHERS:
BLUEPRINTS • PRIMARY COLOURS • LEARNING TARGETS

Stanley Thornes for Teachers publishes practical teacher's ideas books and photocopiable resources for use in primary schools. Our three key series, **Blueprints**, **Primary Colours** and **Learning Targets** together provide busy teachers with unbeatable curriculum coverage, inspiration and value for money. We mail teachers and schools about our books regularly. To join the mailing list simply photocopy and complete the form below and return using the **FREEPOST** address to receive regular updates on our new and existing titles. You may also like to add the name of a friend who would be interested in being on the mailing list. Books can be bought by credit card over the telephone and information obtained on (01242) 267280.

Please add my name to the *Stanley Thornes for* TEACHERS mailing list.

Mr/Mrs/Miss/Ms _____

Address _____

_____ postcode _____

School address _____

_____ postcode _____

Please also send information about *Stanley Thornes for* TEACHERS to:

Mr/Mrs/Miss/Ms _____

Address _____

_____ postcode _____

To: Marketing Services Dept., Stanley Thornes Ltd, FREEPOST (GR 782), Cheltenham, GL50 1BR

Text © Liz Hopkins 1998
Original line illustrations © Stanley Thornes (Publishers) Ltd 1998

First published in 1998 by
Stanley Thornes (Publishers) Ltd
Ellenborough House
Wellington Street
CHELTENHAM GL50 1YW

98 99 00 01 02 / 10 9 8 7 6 5 4 3 2 1

A catalogue record for this book is available from the British Library.

ISBN 0-7487-3583-6

Designed and typeset by John Youé Book Design

Printed and bound in Great Britain
by Redwood Books, Trowbridge, Wiltshire

Contents

Introduction

Blueprints Mental Arithmetic is a carefully structured book, tied to the National Curriculum, offering an interactive approach to improving children's mental facility in mathematics.

It is divided into three sections. The first section covers the five Main Topics of the book with ideas for teaching and copymasters for consolidation. The second section covers three Associated Topics, again with ideas for teaching and copymasters for consolidation, and the final section comprises tests and quick maths copymasters.

How to use this book

Main Topics

The teacher's notes are divided into National Curriculum Levels 1 and 2 and list the copymasters appropriate at each level. The copymasters are grouped together after the teacher's notes.

The teacher's notes covering the five main topics of the book contain a wealth of ideas that can be used with groups or the whole class. The section includes many strategies for learning and each idea and copymaster is clearly linked to the Learning Objectives listed at the start of each topic and in the contents at the start of the section.

The ideas for whole class work are designed to encourage children to take an active part in learning, involving question and answer sessions. It is suggested that these topics are tackled in blocks of one or two weeks, integrating the whole class ideas and the copymasters. Many copymasters are self-explanatory, but some may require additional teacher input.

Associated Topics

The teacher's notes for this section follow the same format as the teacher's notes for the Main Topics. These are followed by copymasters that are ideally suited for individual or group revision of core work.

It is suggested that the copymasters are used a short time after the children have studied a topic in their core mathematics work, hence consolidating and applying their knowledge and understanding. A short mental revision session could be followed by children completing an appropriate copymaster.

Reinforcement and Assessment

There are no teacher's notes as this section provides practice of addition and subtraction and assessment of the work covered in this book. The copymasters are linked to the Learning Objectives listed in the contents at the start of the section.

The topic tests can be used to provide a valuable assessment of the children's grasp of mental arithmetic at regular intervals throughout the year. Having completed a test, you may wish to work through sections of it with small groups or return to some of the ideas for whole class work, or repeat copymasters. Some children may need some support with reading these tests.

The four quick maths copymasters are for practice in speeding up mental addition and subtraction. Most children really enjoy the challenge of beating their personal best. It may be appropriate to remind the children of some of the strategies they have for number work before they attempt a copymaster.

The mental arithmetic tests are written in the style of the end of Key Stage 2 mental arithmetic tests. There are copymaster answer sheets for the children and questions for the teacher to read aloud.

Main Topics

Place Value ▷

Addition ▷

Subtraction ▷

Money ▷

Time ▷

Place Value

LEVEL 1

Learning Objectives

To be able to:
1. Write numbers in words
2. Count to 5
3. Count to 10
4. Order numbers to 10

1 WRITE NUMBERS IN WORDS

C1

Ideas for whole class work
Have two sets of cards with the numbers from 1 to 10 written in words on one set and in numbers on the other set. Have ten children at the front and give them each a number. Hold up a number word and ask the children which child has the matching numeral. Then reverse this and have the children holding the words at the front and choose a child to come out and give a number card to the correct child. Next, try giving all the cards out to the children and get them to find their partner. Ask those without cards to check to see if the numbers and words are paired correctly.

Copymasters
C1 Place Value *Write numbers in words* The words are at the bottom of the sheet so may be left off if you wish.

2 COUNT TO 5

C2

Ideas for whole class work
Choose a child and give them a number from 0 to 5. They need to gather a group of children equal to the number they have been given. Do this with different numbers and children. Do it with cubes, cars, toys and so on, instead of always counting children. Next, use the word cards instead of the number cards.

Copymasters
C2 Place Value *Count to 5*

3 COUNT TO 10

C3-4

Ideas for whole class work
1 You need two sets of cards with the numbers from 1 to 10 written on one set and one to ten objects to count on the other set. Hold up a number card and a counting card and ask the children if they go together. Do this lots of times, sometimes with a matching pair.

2 You need the number and counting cards used above. Stick four counting cards at random on the board. Choose children to come out and choose the correct number card to match a counting card. Do this with several different sets of counting cards. Next, try reversing the process so that the number cards are on the board and the children have to choose the correct counting card.

Copymasters
C3 Place Value *Count to 10*

C4 Place Value *Count to 10*

4 ORDER NUMBERS TO 10

C5

Ideas for whole class work
1 You need the number cards. Choose two children to come out the front. Give one of them a number card. Discuss which numbers are smaller than the number given and which ones are larger. Give the second child a number and get the children to tell you whether it is larger or smaller than the first number. Do this several times. Next, put the children in pairs. Give every child a number card from 1 to 10. Tell them that the child with the smaller number should sit down and the one with the larger number should stand behind them. Check and discuss pairings. This can be done with a mixture of word, number and counting cards.

2 Draw three empty squares on the board. Tell the children that they are going to put three numbers in order of size. Choose a number card and discuss which square to put it in. Once it is placed, it can not be moved. Pick another card and get the children to tell you where to put it compared to the previous number. You may not be able to place it if, for example, the first card was 9 and you put it in the right hand square and then you pick out 10. In this case, discard the second card and pick again. The discussion about where to put the number picked is very valuable and contributes greatly to the understanding of ordering numbers.

Copymasters
C5 Place Value *Order to 10*

Learning Objectives

To be able to:
1. Write numbers in words
2. Count to 20
3. Order numbers to 20 and 100
4. Understand tens and units
5. Add and subtract 10
6. Round to the nearest 10

1 WRITE NUMBERS IN WORDS
C6

Ideas for whole class work
Play Hangman with number names. Choose a child to be out the front to write on the board and then choose children to guess the letters needed to spell the number name on the board. Wrong guesses result in part of the Hangman being drawn.

Copymasters
C6 Place Value *Write numbers to 100 in words*

2 COUNT TO 20
C7

Ideas for whole class work
Split the class into two groups so that each group is less than 20. Choose a member of the group to count how many children are in their group. Then choose another child to check it. Do this several times with different sized groups.

Copymasters
C7 Place Value *Count to 20*

3 ORDER NUMBERS TO 20 AND 100
C8-10

Ideas for whole class work
1 Give each child a number between 1 and 20. Giving the number verbally may be sufficient for some children although others may need a card to see and remember the number. It does not matter if some children have the same number. You say a number out loud or write one on the board. Children with a number less than yours sit down and those with a number greater than yours stand up. Children with the same number as you put their hands up. Check and discuss the children's positions. Do this several times with different numbers. This activity can be repeated for any set of numbers.

2 You need a set of 0 to 100 cards. Pick three at random and get the children to put them in order. Do this for lots of different numbers. Build up to ordering more numbers.

3 You need 0 to 100 cards. Draw ten empty squares in a row on the board. Tell the children you are going to choose numbers and they need to try to put them in order in the squares. Once a number is placed, it can not be moved. Choose a card at random and ask the children to decide which square to put it in. The discussion about where to put it is important. Some numbers may need to be rejected if there is not an appropriate empty square for them. After ten numbers, count up how many you have managed to place correctly. Try again with new numbers. Children can also play this in pairs or in small teams using copymaster C8. They have a row of empty squares, you say the numbers aloud and they choose where to write the number on their sheet. There is a box for numbers they can not place. The winning team is the one with their numbers in the correct order and the fewest numbers in the box.

Copymasters
C8 Place Value *Games* A baseboard for the whole class activity above.

C9 Place Value *Order to 100*

C10 Place Value *Order to 100*

4 UNDERSTAND TENS AND UNITS
C11

Ideas for whole class work
You need squares of two different colours, such as red and blue. Let the red squares equal 10 and the blue squares equal 1. Therefore, two red squares and four blue squares represent 24. Hold up different combinations of the squares and get the children to tell you the numbers they represent. Then, try doing it in reverse. You say a number and choose a child to count out the correct number of red and blue squares.

Copymasters
C11 Place Value *Tens and units to 100*

5 | ADD AND SUBTRACT 10
C12

Ideas for whole class work
On a 1–100 grid, colour a single-digit number red, eg 4. Add 10 to it and colour 14 red. Keep adding 10. Note the pattern and that the units number remains the same. Do this for other start numbers. Next, try starting with a higher number, eg 93, and repeatedly **subtract** 10.

Copymasters
C12 Place Value *Add and subtract 10*

6 | ROUND TO THE NEAREST 10
C13

Ideas for whole class work
You need 0 to 100 cards. To start with, choose two children to stand at the front holding the 0 and 10 cards. Stand the 0 to the left and the 10 to the right as if at either end of a number line. Tell the children that you are a number between 0 and 10, for example 7. Start at 0 and walk slowly towards 10. Get the children to tell you when to stop in order to be in the right place for 7. Do this for other numbers and other number lines. Teach the children that if the units number is 5, it always rounds up to the next ten.

Copymasters
C13 Place Value *Round to nearest 10*

Addition

LEVEL 1

Learning Objectives
To be able to:
1. Add numbers up to 5
2. Add 1 or 2 more
3. Add numbers up to 10
4. Use addition to solve problems

1 | ADD NUMBERS UP TO 5
C14

Ideas for whole class work
Use five children at the front to show the partitions of five: 0 + 5, 1 + 4, 2 + 3, etc. Show how the different groupings can be written as addition sums. Count out five cubes. Have some in one hand and some in the other. Open one hand to reveal the cubes and get children to tell you how many cubes are hidden in the other hand. You could use a bag and get a child to pick some cubes out of the bag and ask the children how many are left in the bag. Encourage the children to explain their answers to develop their language and understanding.

Copymasters
C14 Addition *Add numbers up to 5*

2 | ADD 1 OR 2 MORE
C15-16

Ideas for whole class work
1 You need ten cubes and a cloth or small bag. Choose a child to come and put some cubes, between one and eight, in the bag or under the cloth. Get them to hold up the appropriate number card. Get another child to come and put one more cube into the bag. Ask the children how many cubes they think are in the bag now. Count the cubes to check. Do this several times. This activity can also be used for adding 2 more.

2 You need number cards 0 to 10 and ten cubes. Hold up a number card from 1 to 8 and choose a child to count out the correct number of cubes. Choose another child to add one more cube, count how many there are altogether and pick the corresponding number card. Eventually, the children will be able to do this without counting all the cubes but just by adding 1 to the first number. This activity can also be used for adding 2 more.

Copymasters
C15 Addition *Add 1 more*

C16 Addition *Add 2 more*

3 ADD NUMBERS UP TO 10
C17-18

Ideas for whole class work
1 Work towards quick-fire answers by firstly adding 1 to any number you say, then move on to adding 2. Children enjoy playing Fingers Up. Either say a number aloud or show the children a number card, then say, for example 'add 3'. The children have to hold up the number of fingers equal to the answer. This can be played with eyes closed for quick and easy assessment of adding numbers up to 10.

2 Teach the children that when adding two numbers it is easier to store the bigger number in your head then add on the smaller number. Give them sums to do out loud and get the children to explain how they worked them out. For example: 6 + 2, store the 6 in your head then count on 2 more.

3 It is important that children really learn their addition facts of 10. Get the children to give you pairs of numbers that add to make 10. You could use ten children or cubes to help if necessary. Write the sums on the board. Get the children to help you to list the sums in order and then look for patterns. Show that as one number increases, the other number decreases.

Copymasters
C17 Addition *Add numbers up to 10*

C18 Addition *Add numbers up to 10*

4 USE ADDITION TO SOLVE PROBLEMS
C19

Ideas for whole class work
Give a child two numbers and get them to make up a number problem for the other children to answer. Choose a child to write the sum on the board.

Copymasters
C19 Addition *Addition to solve problems*

LEVEL 2

Learning objectives
To be able to:
1. Recall mentally addition facts of 10
2. Add numbers up to 20
3. Use addition to solve problems

---

1 RECALL MENTALLY ADDITION FACTS OF 10
C20-21

Ideas for whole class work
1 Write the numbers 1 to 10 on the board in a random fashion. Point to two of the numbers and choose a child to say simply 'Yes' if they add to 10 or 'No' if they do not. Do this several times. Next, get the children to close their eyes. You say aloud two numbers and if they add to 10 the children have to put up a hand. This can be an easy assessment of their grasp of the addition facts of 10.

2 Give each child a number from 0 to 10. You could give them a number card or just tell them the number. You hold up a number card from 0 to 10, or say a number aloud, and the children have to identify whether their number added to your number makes 10. If it does, they have to hold up their number card or stand up. Work towards doing this at speed. It can be good fun and it can be played over and over again, giving the children different numbers.

3 Once children know their number facts of 10, encourage them to use them to work out other sums. Write a sum that makes 9 on the board and choose a child to give the answer and explain how they did it by using number facts of 10. For example: 4 + 5 = 9, because 5 + 5 = 10 so it must be 1 less, or 4 + 6 = 10 so it must be 1 less. Next, try doing sums that make 11 and again use facts of 10 to help. For example: 7 + 4 = 11, because 7 + 3 = 10, so it must be 1 more.

Copymasters
C20 Addition *Addition facts of 10*

C21 Addition *Addition facts of 10*

2 ADD NUMBERS UP TO 20
C22-26

Ideas for whole class work
1 If the children learn the answers to doubles these can be used to help with other addition sums. It can also support work on even numbers. Have towers of cubes ready at the front, two of each number from 1 to 10. Choose a child to come out and show you double 3. They need to pick up the two 3 towers and say 'Double 3 is 6'. Do this several times and gradually the children will give you the answer without picking out the towers.

2 Give the children 'near doubles' to work out and get them to explain how they used the double to help. For example: 7 + 8 = 15, because 7 + 7 is 14, it must be 1 more.

3 Firstly, practise adding 10 to single digit numbers until the children are sure that the units digit stays the same. Then encourage them to use this knowledge to add on 9. For example: 5 + 9 = 14, because 5 + 10 = 15, it must be 1 less.

Copymasters
C22 Addition *Add numbers: up to 20* Use doubles.

C23 Addition *Add numbers: up to 20* This sheet is designed to be used several times. Give the children the number to be added to each of the four sets of numbers.

C24 Addition *Add numbers: up to 20* Sums in words to be answered in words.

C25 Addition *Add numbers: up to 20* Making 18 and 19.

C26 Addition *Add numbers: up to 20* Adding 10 or 9.

3 | USE ADDITION TO SOLVE PROBLEMS
C27

Ideas for whole class work
The children work individually on the copymaster.

Copymasters
C27 Addition *Addition to solve problems*

Subtraction

LEVEL **1**	**Learning Objectives**

Learning Objectives

To be able to:
1. Count back
2. Subtract numbers up to 5
3. Work out 1 less
4. Subtract numbers up to 10
5. Use subtraction to solve problems

It is important to explicitly tackle subtraction as take away, counting back, difference and complement.

1 | COUNT BACK
C28

Ideas for whole class work
Give out the number cards 0 to 5. Get the child with the 5 to come out the front and hold up their card. Ask who should come next if the numbers are to count backwards. Continue to 0. Try starting at other numbers. Next, try doing it without the cards, choosing children to say the numbers to count backwards.

Copymasters
C28 Subtraction *Count back*

2 | SUBTRACT NUMBERS UP TO 5
C29

Ideas for whole class work
Put the children into small groups and give each group

five cubes or have the children in groups of five. Hold up a number card from 0 to 5. Children have to take that number away from their five cubes and hold up the number of cubes that are left. You may wish the children to hold up fingers instead of cubes so that they are all actively involved.

Copymasters
C29 Subtraction *Subtract numbers: up to 5*

3 | WORK OUT 1 LESS
C30

Ideas for whole class work
Show the children a number of cubes. Get one of them to hold up the correct number card. Ask another child to come and take one away from your cubes, count how many are left and select the corresponding number card. Next, try plotting a point on the number line from 0 to 10 and ask a child to plot the point 1 less.

Copymasters
C30 Subtraction *Work out 1 less*

4 SUBTRACT NUMBERS UP TO 10
C31-32

Ideas for whole class work
1 Practise doing simple subtraction sums.
(i) Focus on counting back as a way of working them out. Get the children to explain how they did the sum. For example: 8 – 5, I started on 8 and counted back 5 (7, 6, 5, 4, 3) so the answer is 3. Use a number line.
(ii) Next, show them that the difference between the two numbers is also the answer. A number line can be very useful for this. Choose children to come and show how they worked out the sum using the number line. Also, use one-to-one matching to show the difference between two sets of cubes.
(iii) Use fingers or cubes to practise taking away as a method of working out subtraction sums.
(iv) Focus on counting on as a way of working out the complement. For example: use 5 + 3 = 8 to work out 8 – 5 = 3. Draw a set of circles on the board and draw a line separating it into two groups. Get the children to tell the number story. For example: a set of eight circles with a line splitting it into three and five. 'I had eight, take away five leaves three.'

2 Have the numbers 0 to 10 arranged at random on the board. Decide on a difference and choose a child to come out and select two cards with that difference. For exam-

ple, difference of 3: the child may choose 2 and 5. Keep the difference the same and get other children to pick pairs of cards with that difference. When no more pairs are possible, arrange the pairs selected in order and notice that as one number decreases so does the other. Next, do this for other differences.

Copymasters
C31 Subtraction *Subtract numbers: up to 10* Find the difference between two number cards.

C32 Subtraction *Subtract numbers: up to 10* Count and then take away 3 or 4.

5 USE SUBTRACTION TO SOLVE PROBLEMS
C33

Ideas for whole class work
Ask the children a subtraction problem. For example: I had six sweets and I gave two away; how many are left? Choose a child to show how to work out the answer using cubes. Choose another child to construct the sum with number cards or write it on the board. Do this for lots of other number problems.

Copymasters
C33 Subtraction *Subtraction to solve problems*

LEVEL 2

Learning Objectives

To be able to:
1. Recall mentally subtraction up to 10
2. Subtract numbers up to 20
3. Use subtraction to solve problems

---

1 RECALL MENTALLY SUBTRACTION UP TO 10
C34-35

Ideas for whole class work
1 Practise subtraction sums where the answer is half the number. Vary the language you use: 8 take away 4; subtract 4 from 8; what is the difference between 4 and 8; and so on. Work on speed as well as accuracy so that if you say 10, for example, they can reply take away 5, leaves 5.

2 Have two children at the front. One with the number cards 0 to 5, the other with the number cards 6 to 10. Get them each to select a card at random and show them to the class. Choose a child to give the difference between the two numbers, explaining how they worked it out. For some children the answer to how they worked it out will be 'I just knew'.

3 A quick-fire game to make subtraction to 10 fun. Give each child a number between 0 and 10, either on a card

or verbally. Say a number between 0 and 10 and the children have to take that number away from 10. If their number is the answer, they stand up and say it aloud. You may want to focus on certain pairs that make 10 during a session, for example 10 – 3, 10 – 4, 10 – 6 and so only give out a particular selection of numbers, in this case 7, 6 and 4. You could try giving some children two numbers to remember.

Copymasters
C34 Subtraction *Subtraction up to 10*

C35 Subtraction *Subtraction up to 10*

2 SUBTRACT NUMBERS UP TO 20
C36-38

Ideas for whole class work
1 It is very useful if the children know the doubles to 20,

9 + 9, 6 + 6 and so on. These can be used to speed up subtraction. Start by using towers of cubes, one for each of the even numbers from 10 to 20. Ask a question such as 18 – 9 and choose a child to show the answer using the cubes. Note that the cubes taken away are equal to the cubes left. Put the tower back together showing that 9 + 9 = 18. Do this for the other numbers. Some children may find it helpful to note the link with the 2× table.

2 Children need to be taught to use their number facts of 10 to work out sums using bigger numbers. Divide the class into two teams. One team will subtract from 10, the other team will subtract from 20. You write a number between 1 and 10 on the board and the teams subtract it from their given number. Write their answers in two columns next to your number. Do this several times. Spot the links between them.

3 You need two sets of cards. One set from 10 to 19, the other set from 0 to 9. Shuffle the two sets and pick one from each. In pairs, the children have to work out the difference and, on a command from you, hold up the correct number of fingers. The children need to be in pairs or they will not have enough fingers for some of the answers.

Copymasters
C36 Subtraction *Subtract numbers: up to 20* Use doubles.

C37 Subtraction *Subtract numbers: up to 20* Links with subtraction facts of 10.

C38 Subtraction *Subtract numbers: up to 20* Identify differences of 7 and 8.

3 USE SUBTRACTION TO SOLVE PROBLEMS
C39

Ideas for whole class work
The children work individually on the copymaster.

Copymasters
C39 Subtraction *Subtraction to solve problems*

Money

LEVEL 1

Learning Objectives

To be able to:
1. Recognize 1p, 2p, 5p and 10p coins
2. Make amounts using coins
3. Add up to 10p
4. Subtract up to 10p
5. Solve problems using addition and subtraction

1 RECOGNIZE 1p, 2p, 5p AND 10p COINS
C40-41

Ideas for whole class work
Have a selection of coins at the front and choose children to come out and pick up a particular coin to show to the class. Start with just 1p and 2p coins, then add 5p and 10p coins. Next, ask a child to come and count out, for example, three 2p coins or two 5p coins. Hold up a coin and ask 'What is this?'. Practise this until the children are very familiar with the different coins.

Copymasters
C40 Money *Recognize coins: 1p, 2p*

C41 Money *Recognize coins: 1p, 2p, 5p, 10p*

2 MAKE AMOUNTS USING COINS
C42-43

Ideas for whole class work
1 Have a pile of pennies at the front. Choose children to come and count out amounts of money up to 10p. Next, have a pile with four 2p coins and three 1p coins. Ask a child to come and count out, for example, 7p. Record the way they do it on the board. Challenge the children to make up 7p in a different way. Do this for other amounts up to 10p. Vary the coins available. Next, include 5p coins in the selection.

2 Put the children in small groups either with pencil and paper or with access to coins as appropriate. Tell them to make an amount of money, for example 8p, in as many different ways as they can, as quickly as they can. Tell them when to start and stop. Get the groups to swap and check each other's work. Ask the children to say some ways out loud and check them using coins if necessary.

Copymasters

C42 Money *Make amounts using coins* Amounts up to 6p.

C43 Money *Make amounts using coins* Amounts up to 10p.

3	ADD UP TO 10p

C44

Ideas for whole class work
Have two sets of cards labelled from 1p to 5p at the front. Select a card from each set. Hold up the cards and the children have to add the two amounts. If necessary, choose a child to come and count out the two lots of money and another child to count how much there is altogether. Do this lots of times with different amounts.

Copymasters
C44 Money *Add up to 10p*

4	SUBTRACT UP TO 10p

C45

Ideas for whole class work
Have two sets of cards, one set from 1p to 5p, the other set from 6p to 10p. Select a card from each set. Hold up the two amounts and the children have to find the difference between the two amounts. Vary the language you use. What is the difference between 7p and 3p? If I have 7p and I spend 3p, how much have I left? How much less than 7p is 3p? If I have 3p and I need 7p, how much more do I need?

Copymasters
C45 Money *Subtract up to 10p*

5	SOLVE PROBLEMS USING ADDITION AND SUBTRACTION

C46-47

Ideas for whole class work
Have a set of cards from 0 to 10p. Select two cards and choose a child to make up a money problem. For example, if the cards selected were 5 and 3 the child may say something like 'I spent 3p then I spent 5p, how much did I spend altogether?' Or 'I had 5p and I spent 3p, how much did I have left?'. The child then chooses another child to give the answer and the first child must say whether the answer is correct or not. The second child now picks two cards from the pack and makes up a new money problem.

Copymasters
C46 Money *Solve problems: add/subtract*

C47 Money *Solve problems: add/subtract* Work out the change from 10p.

LEVEL 2	**Learning Objectives**

To be able to:
1. Recognize all coins
2. Make amounts using coins
3. Add up to 20p
4. Subtract up to 20p
5. Solve problems using money

1	RECOGNIZE ALL COINS

Ideas for whole class work
Have a small bag at the front with a selection of coins in it. Choose a child to come out and put their hand into the bag. Tell them to feel a coin and see if they can say what it is, then bring it out of the bag to check. Vary the selection of coins you put in the bag. Next, try challenging the children to pick out a particular coin by feel alone.

Copymasters
None.

2	MAKE AMOUNTS USING COINS

C48-49

Ideas for whole class work
1 Teach the children to make amounts up by starting with the largest coin possible. Focus on just identifying the largest coin at first. For example: what is the largest coin I can use if I want 17p? – a 10p coin; 24p? – a 20p coin; 36p? – a 20p coin. Move on to identifying how much is left. For example: 17p – a 10p coin and 7p left.

2 Select five coins and write or draw them on the board, for example, 1p, 1p, 2p, 5p and 5p. Challenge the children to make different amounts using only those coins. Do this for other combinations of coins.

3 Select five coins and write or draw them on the board, for example, 1p, 1p, 2p, 5p and 5p. Ask questions such as 'What is the largest amount I can make using only three coins?', 'What is the smallest amount I can make using four coins?', 'Can you make eight pence?'. Do this for other combinations of coins.

Copymasters

C48 Money *Make amounts using coins*

C49 Money *Make amounts using coins*

3	ADD UP TO 20p
C50–52	

Ideas for whole class work
Have a selection of coins at the front. Get a child to select any five coins with a total value less than 20p and tell the class the chosen coins. For example, two 5p coins and three 2p coins. The class has to work out how much money the child chose, in this case 16p, and the child has to tell them if they are correct.

Copymasters

C50 Money *Add up to 20p* The copymaster has four sets of money. Tell the children how much to add to each set. Answers are given for set A, 8p; set B, 6p; set C, 10p; set D, 9p. This sheet is designed to be used several times.

C51 Money *Add up to 20p*

C52 Money *Add up to 20p*

4	SUBTRACT UP TO 20p
C53	

Ideas for whole class work
Have a set of cards from 1p to 20p. Turn over a card and get the children to work out how much change they would get from 20p if the amount on the card represents what they spent. Aim for speed and accuracy. You may want to ask the children from which coins the change could be made up.

Copymasters
C53 Money *Subtract up to 20p*

5	SOLVE PROBLEMS USING MONEY
C54	

Ideas for whole class work
The children work individually on the copymaster.

Copymasters
C54 Money *Solve problems using money*

Time

LEVEL 1	**Learning Objectives**

To be able to:
1. Sequence events and develop language
2. Identify days of the week
3. Tell the time using o'clock

1	SEQUENCE EVENTS AND DEVELOP LANGUAGE

Ideas for whole class work
1 You need some pictures showing events. Ask the children what might have happened just before the event or just after the event.

2 Discuss what the children did before coming to school. Ask them what they will be doing after school. Talk about before and after lunchtime and so on.

3 Talk about which comes first with daily events: get dressed, wake up, get out of bed. Which comes last: eat tea, cook tea, wash the dishes. Ask the children to give an event which would come before, for example, arriving at school, eating lunch, getting home, going to sleep, and so on. Do the same for events that come after these.

Copymasters
None.

2	IDENTIFY DAYS OF THE WEEK
C55	

Ideas for whole class work
Find out what children do on different days of the week,

either using the children's home activities or school activities or clubs. For example, on Monday we have 'sharing time', on Tuesday we do PE, and so on. Have cards with the days of the week written on them and get children to hold the cards and stand in order. Then do it missing out one of the days. Ask the children which day is missing. Discuss which day comes before or after another.

Copymasters
C55 Time *Days of the week*

3 TELL THE TIME USING O'CLOCK
C56-57

Ideas for whole class work
1 You need a large clockface. Cover up one of the numbers and ask the children which number is covered. Then cover two numbers. Ask which numbers come before or after another number.

2 You need a large clockface and a digital clock. Move the hands to show, for example, nine o'clock and ask the children what happens at that time of the day. At the same time, show 9:00 on the digital clock. Do the same for other times. You may wish to discuss whether it is morning or evening.

3 You need a large clockface and a digital clock. Move the hands to show, for example, six o'clock and choose a child to put the digital clock to the same time. Do this the other way around as well. Next, get the child to show the time an hour before or after your time.

Copymasters
C56 Time *Tell the time using o'clock*

C57 Time *Tell the time: analogue/digital*

LEVEL 2

Learning Objectives

To:
1. Know days of the week, months of the year
2. Tell the time using half past, quarter to and past
3. Know minutes and hours
4. Work out duration

1 KNOW DAYS OF THE WEEK, MONTHS OF THE YEAR
C58-59

Ideas for whole class work
1 Ask questions such as what day is it tomorrow, what day was it yesterday, what is the day in three days time, and so on.

2 Learn the months of the year in order. Go round the class saying the months aloud, choosing a different child for each month. Next, say a month aloud and ask a child what month comes next or what month came before it. Try saying some months aloud in order but miss one out. For example, May, June, August. The children have to tell you which month was missed out.

Copymasters
C58 Time *Days of the week* Yesterday and the day after tomorrow.

C59 Time *Months of the year* Order the months.

2 TELL THE TIME USING HALF PAST, QUARTER TO AND PAST
C60-61

Ideas for whole class work
1 Have the children in pairs. One of the children is the clock and the other one sets the time. Say a time aloud and the time-setter must move the arms of the 'clock' to show the given time. Use a straight arm for the minute hand and a bent arm for the hour hand. After several times, the children swap roles.

2 You need a clockface and digital display. Choose two children to come out and quietly tell them a time to display on their clocks. They show their times to the class, after you have checked that they are correct, and choose a child to tell them the time in two different ways, for example, six fifteen and quarter past six.

Copymasters
C60 Time *Tell the time: analogue/digital*

C61 Time *Tell the time: analogue/digital*

3 KNOW MINUTES AND HOURS

C62

Ideas for whole class work

Practise changing half, quarter and three-quarters of an hour into minutes. Use a clock face and digital display to show the comparison of quarter hour and 15 minutes.

Copymasters

C62 Time *Know minutes and hours*

4 WORK OUT DURATION

C63-64

Ideas for whole class work

1 You need a clockface and digital display. Set the two clocks an hour apart and ask how long it is from one time to the other. Do this for other times. Use times such as half past two and quarter to three and work on giving the answer as a fraction of an hour and in minutes.

2 You need a clockface and digital display. Set one clock to a time and ask a child to come and set the other clock to the time, for example, half an hour later, quarter of an hour earlier and so on. Use fractions of an hour and minutes so that the children become secure in the knowledge that quarter of an hour is 15 minutes and so on.

Copymasters

C63 Time *Duration*

C64 Time *Duration*

Name _____

Date _____

Write the numbers in words

3

— — — — —

7

— — — — —

1

— — —

10

— — —

6

— — —

8

— — — — —

9

— — — —

5

— — — —

2

— — —

4

— — — —

one	two	three	four	five
six	seven	eight	nine	ten

Name

Date

How many?

Set A

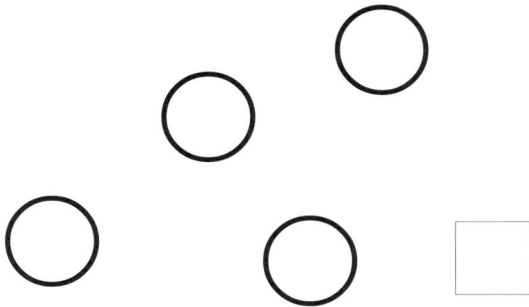

Set B

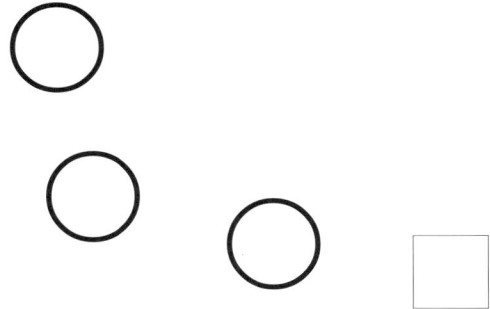

Set C

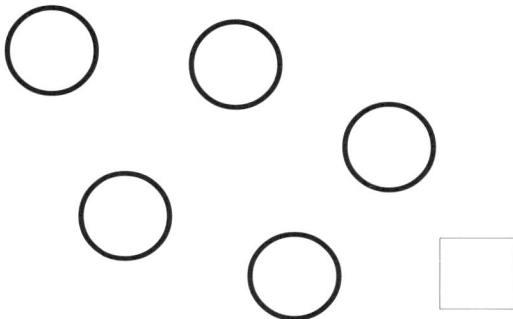

Set D

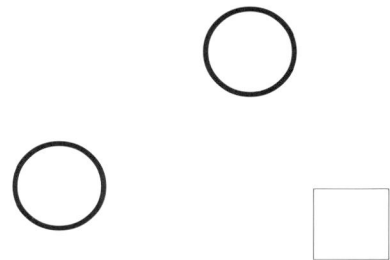

Set E

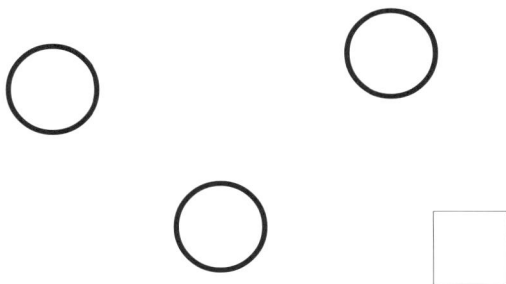

Set F

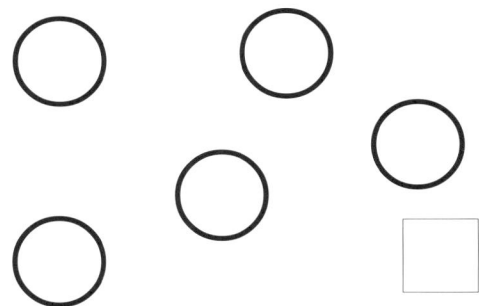

Set G

Set H

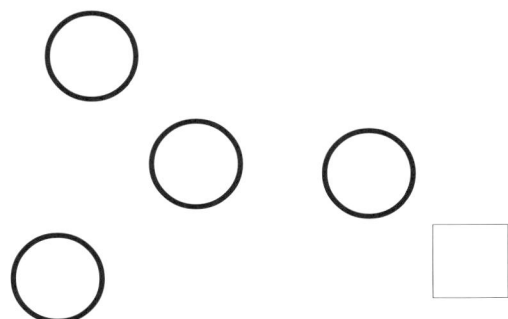

Name_____

Date_____

How many?

Set A

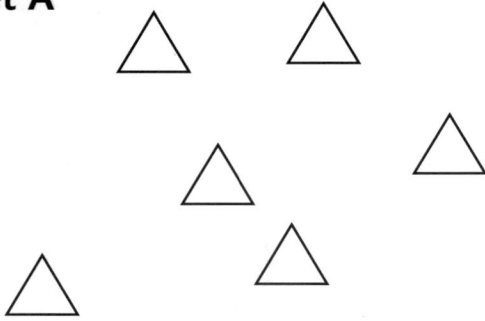

Set B

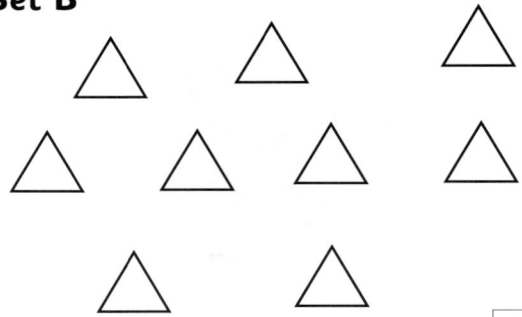

Set C

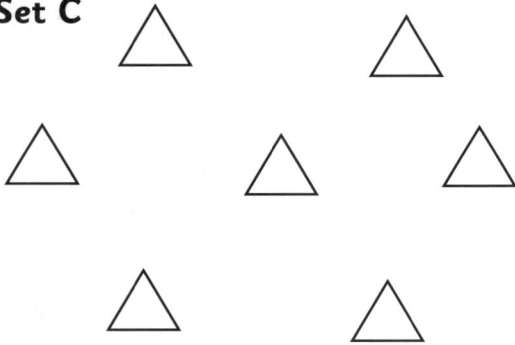

Set D

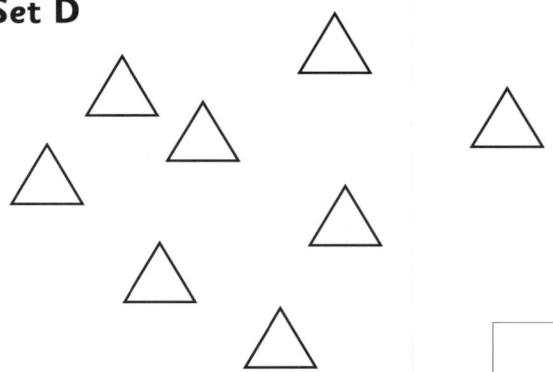

Set E

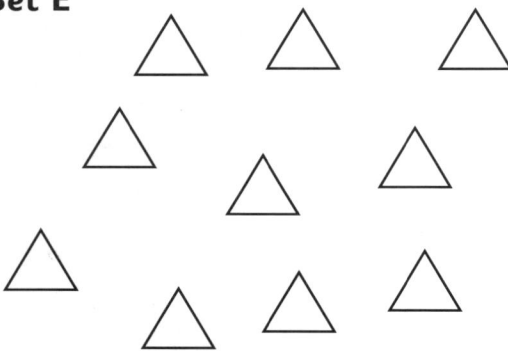

Set F

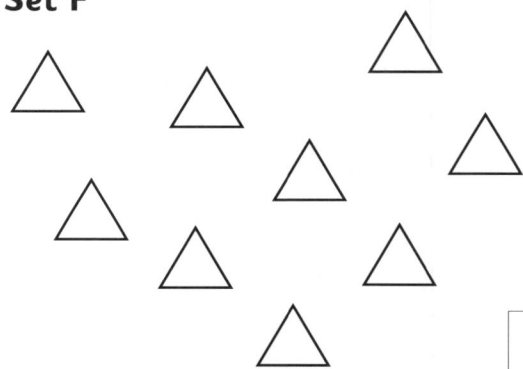

Set G

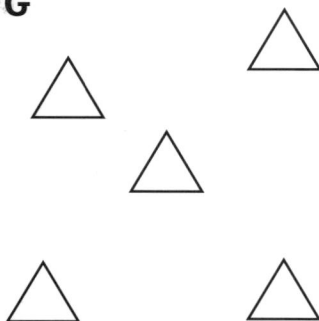

Set H

Name _____

Date _____

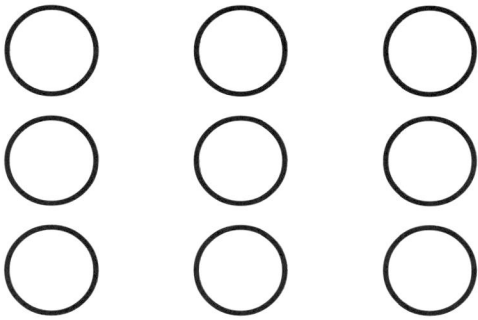

Colour five

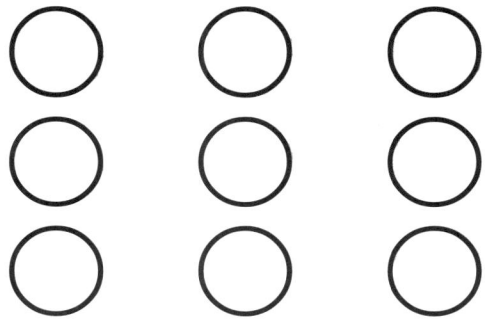

Colour eight

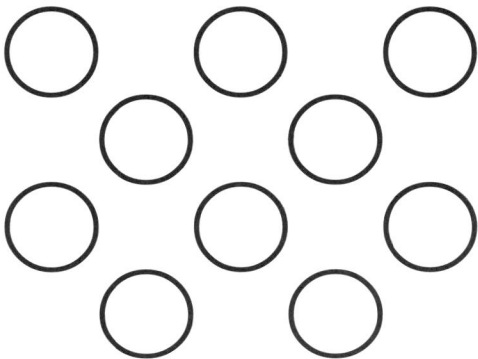

Colour seven

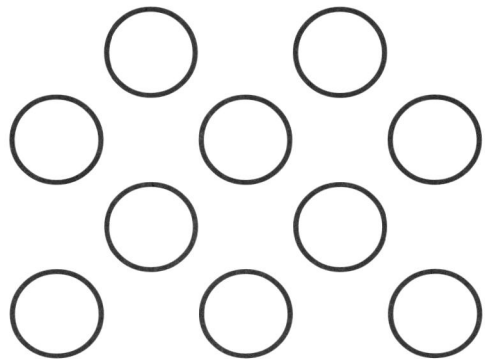

Colour six

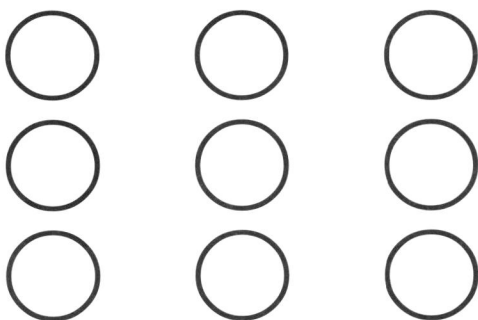

Colour nine

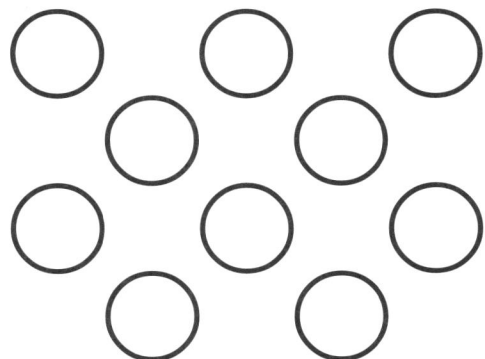

Colour eight

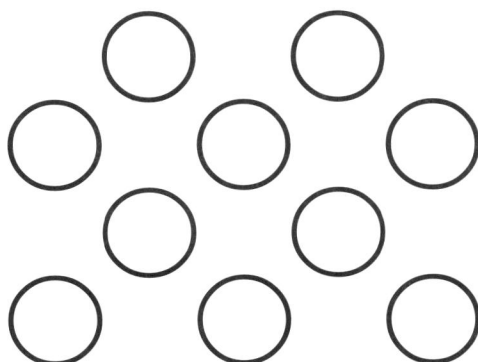

Colour ten

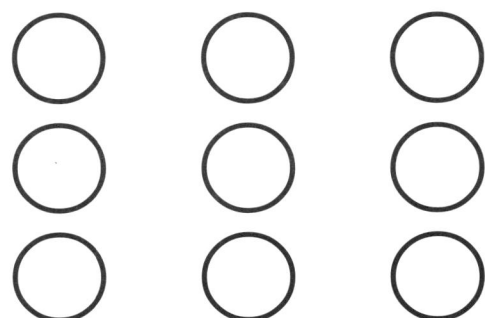

Colour seven

Name

Date

Colour the highest number each time

1 | 3 | 9 | 4 |

2 | 2 | 1 | 3 |

3 | 8 | 3 | 7 |

4 | 5 | 4 | 6 |

5 | 10 | 9 | 7 |

6 | 4 | 3 | 6 | 5 |

7 | 6 | 8 | 5 | 7 |

8 | 1 | 3 | 6 |

9 | 9 | 7 | 4 |

10 | 5 | 10 | 8 |

11 | 4 | 1 | 5 |

12 | 7 | 8 | 6 |

13 | 7 | 10 | 8 | 9 |

14 | 9 | 6 | 8 | 5 |

Name

Date

Write in words

1   72   _____

2   58   _____

3   35   _____

4   40   _____

5   89   _____

6   100 _____

7   61   _____

8   27   _____

9   93   _____

10 46   _____

Name_____

Date_____

How many?

Set A

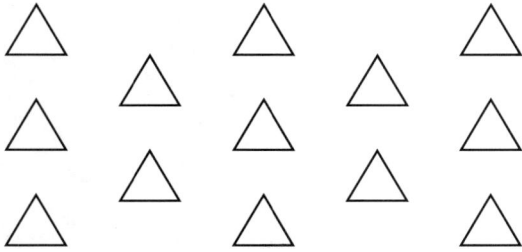

Set B

Set C

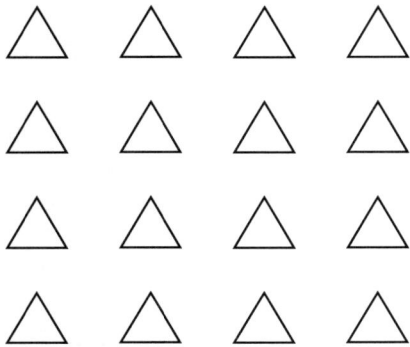

Set D

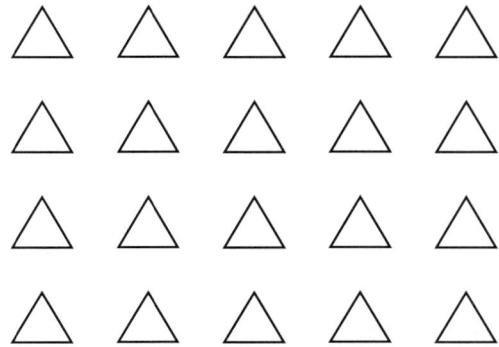

Set E

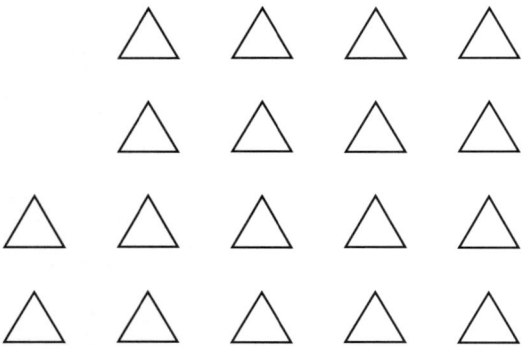

Set F

Set G

Set H

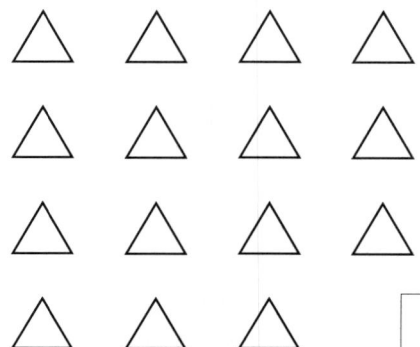

Name

Date

Game 1

Numbers left out

Game 2

Numbers left out

Name _____

Date _____

Fill in the missing numbers

1 | 18 | 19 | | | 22 | | 24 | |

2 | 37 | 38 | | | 42 | | | |

3 | 66 | 67 | | | | | 72 | |

4 | | 89 | | | 93 | | | |

5 | | 47 | 48 | | | 52 | | |

6 | | | | 81 | 82 | | 84 | |

7 | | 70 | | 72 | 73 | | | |

8 | | | | | | 91 | 92 | |

Name_____

Date_____

Put the numbers in order, smallest first

1   21   17   27   30   →   ☐ ☐ ☐ ☐

2   36   24   41   40   →   ☐ ☐ ☐ ☐

3   19   11   23   20   →   ☐ ☐ ☐ ☐

4   31   21   13   16   →   ☐ ☐ ☐ ☐

5   47   37   27   30   →   ☐ ☐ ☐ ☐

6   53   49   35   50   →   ☐ ☐ ☐ ☐

7   71   61   69   70   →   ☐ ☐ ☐ ☐

8   35   56   41   68   →   ☐ ☐ ☐ ☐

9   99   89   90   19   →   ☐ ☐ ☐ ☐

10   79   86   97   68   →   ☐ ☐ ☐ ☐

Name _____

Date _____

How many tens? How many units?

1   Seventy-three   =   ☐ tens   ☐ units

2   Ninety-five   =   ☐ tens   ☐ units

3   Sixty-two   =   ☐ tens   ☐ units

4   Fifty-four   =   ☐ tens   ☐ units

5   Thirty-eight   =   ☐ tens   ☐ units

6   Eighty-six   =   ☐ tens   ☐ units

7   Forty-seven   =   ☐ tens   ☐ units

8   Twenty-one   =   ☐ tens   ☐ units

9   Ninety-nine   =   ☐ tens   ☐ units

10   Eighty   =   ☐ tens   ☐ units

Name

Date

Fill in the missing numbers

1	2	12	22	32	☐	☐	62
2	29	39	☐	59	☐	☐	89
3	4	☐	24	34	☐	☐	64
4	75	65	55	☐	☐	25	15
5	93	83	☐	☐	53	☐	33
6	5	☐	25	35	☐	☐	65
7	7	☐	☐	37	47	☐	☐
8	40	50	☐	70	☐	☐	☐
9	98	88	☐	☐	58	☐	☐
10	61	51	☐	☐	21	☐	☐

Plot the number on the line. What is the nearest 10?

1   8      Nearest 10 is [   ]

2   12      Nearest 10 is [   ]

3   27      Nearest 10 is [   ]

4   54      Nearest 10 is [   ]

5   48      Nearest 10 is [   ]

6   72      Nearest 10 is [   ]

7   86      Nearest 10 is [   ]

8   63      Nearest 10 is [   ]

9   75      Nearest 10 is [   ]

10   35      Nearest 10 is [   ]

Name

Date

Work out the sums

1   4 + 1 = ☐   **7**   2 + 3 = ☐

2   2 + 2 = ☐   **8**   1 + 2 = ☐

3   1 + 3 = ☐   **9**   3 + 0 = ☐

4   2 + 1 = ☐   **10**   1 + 4 = ☐

5   3 + 2 = ☐   **11**   3 + 1 = ☐

6   5 + 0 = ☐   **12**   0 + 4 = ☐

Write three sums that make 5	Write three sums that make 4
1 ☐ + ☐ = 5	**1** ☐ + ☐ = 4
2 ☐ + ☐ = 5	**2** ☐ + ☐ = 4
3 ☐ + ☐ = 5	**3** ☐ + ☐ = 4

Name_____

Date_____

How many? Add 1 more

1 ●●●●●● ☐ ● 1 more makes ☐

2 ○○○○○ ☐ ○ 1 more makes ☐

3 ●●●●● ●●●● ☐ ● 1 more makes ☐

4 ○○○○ ☐ ○ 1 more makes ☐

5 ●●●● ●●● ☐ ● 1 more makes ☐

6 ○○○ ☐ ○ 1 more makes ☐

7 ●●●● ●●●● ☐ ● 1 more makes ☐

8 ○○○ ○○○ ☐ ○ 1 more makes ☐

9 ●●●● ☐ ● 1 more makes ☐

10 ○○○○○ ○○○○ ☐ ○ 1 more makes ☐

28

Name _____

Date _____

How many triangles? Add 2 to each set. Now how many?

Set A

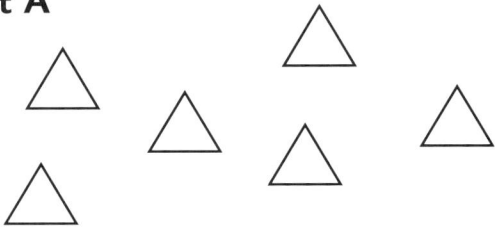

☐ + 2 = ☐

Set B

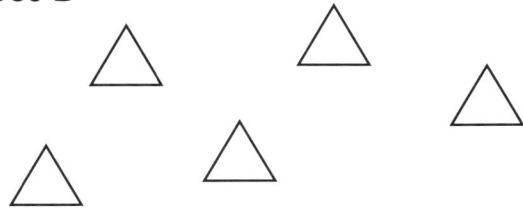

☐ + 2 = ☐

Set C

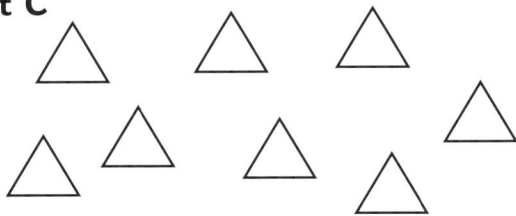

☐ + 2 = ☐

Set D

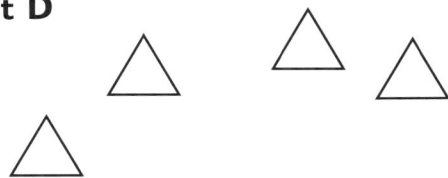

☐ + 2 = ☐

Set E

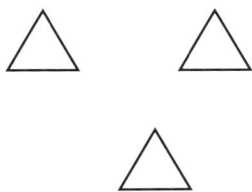

☐ + 2 = ☐

Set F

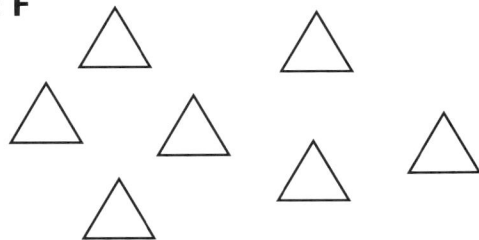

☐ + 2 = ☐

Set G

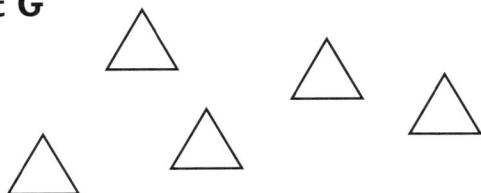

☐ + 2 = ☐

Set H

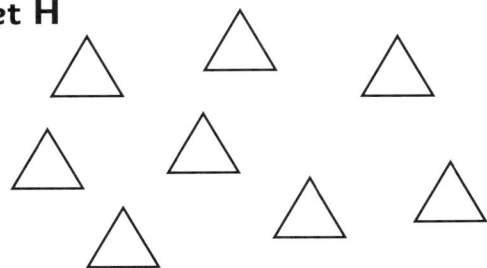

☐ + 2 = ☐

Name _____

Date _____

How many circles? Add 3 to each set. Now how many?

Set A	Set B	Set C
	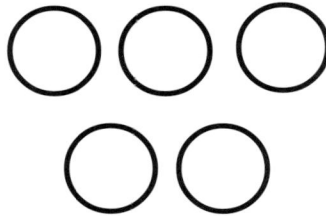	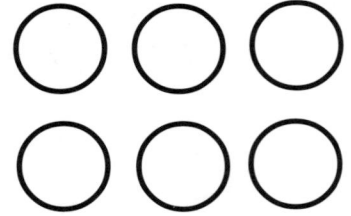
☐ + 3 = ☐	☐ + 3 = ☐	☐ + 3 = ☐

Set D	Set E	Set F
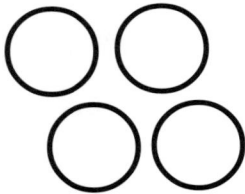		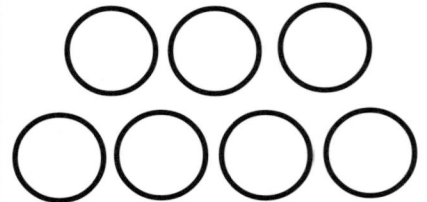
☐ + 3 = ☐	☐ + 3 = ☐	☐ + 3 = ☐

How many triangles? Add 4 to each set. Now how many?

Set G	Set H	Set I
		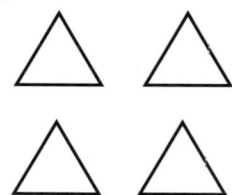
☐ + 4 = ☐	☐ + 4 = ☐	☐ + 4 = ☐

Name _____

Date _____

Work out the sums

1   5 + 3 = ☐   **7**   5 + 5 = ☐

2   3 + 4 = ☐   **8**   6 + 4 = ☐

3   6 + 2 = ☐   **9**   7 + 2 = ☐

4   4 + 4 = ☐   **10**   5 + 4 = ☐

5   3 + 7 = ☐   **11**   3 + 6 = ☐

6   6 + 3 = ☐   **12**   2 + 8 = ☐

Write six sums that make 10

1   ☐ + ☐ = 10   **4**   ☐ + ☐ = 10

2   ☐ + ☐ = 10   **5**   ☐ + ☐ = 10

3   ☐ + ☐ = 10   **6**   ☐ + ☐ = 10

Name_____

Date_____

How many altogether?

1   5 sweets   3 more sweets   ☐ + ☐ = ☐

2   6 marbles   Add 2 more   ☐ + ☐ = ☐

3   4 shells   Find 3 more   ☐ + ☐ = ☐

4   8 biscuits   Add 2 more   ☐ + ☐ = ☐

5   3 cars   6 more cars   ☐ + ☐ = ☐

6   5 bikes   Add 4 more   ☐ + ☐ = ☐

7   4 bags   6 more bags   ☐ + ☐ = ☐

8   7 eggs   3 more eggs   ☐ + ☐ = ☐

9   2 bricks   Add 7 more   ☐ + ☐ = ☐

10   5 flowers   Pick 5 more   ☐ + ☐ = ☐

Name

Date

Put a ring around sums that make 10

4 + 6   3 + 7   8 + 1

9 + 1   5 + 4

2 + 7   3 + 6   5 + 4

4 + 5   1 + 9

7 + 3   5 + 5   8 + 2

6 + 5   3 + 5

2 + 8   10 + 0   6 + 3

Name _____

Date _____

1 Use 7 + 3 = 10 to work out

7 + 4 = ☐   6 + 3 = ☐   8 + 3 = ☐

2 Use 2 + 8 = 10 to work out

3 + 8 = ☐   2 + 9 = ☐   2 + 7 = ☐

3 Use 5 + 5 = 10 to work out

4 + 5 = ☐   5 + 6 = ☐   5 + 4 = ☐

4 Use 6 + 4 = 10 to work out

6 + 3 = ☐   7 + 4 = ☐   6 + 5 = ☐

5 Use 8 + 2 = 10 to work out

7 + 2 = ☐   8 + 3 = ☐   9 + 2 = ☐

6 Use 3 + 7 = 10 to work out

4 + 7 = ☐   2 + 7 = ☐   3 + 8 = ☐

Name

Date

Use 'doubles' to work out the sums

1 6 + 6 = ☐   5 + 6 = ☐   7 + 6 = ☐

2 4 + 4 = ☐   3 + 4 = ☐   4 + 5 = ☐

3 9 + 9 = ☐   9 + 10 = ☐   8 + 9 = ☐

4 3 + 3 = ☐   4 + 3 = ☐   3 + 4 = ☐

5 7 + 7 = ☐   7 + 6 = ☐   8 + 7 = ☐

6 5 + 5 = ☐   4 + 5 = ☐   5 + 6 = ☐

7 9 + 9 = ☐   9 + 8 = ☐   10 + 9 = ☐

8 8 + 8 = ☐   7 + 8 = ☐   9 + 8 = ☐

9 6 + 6 = ☐   7 + 6 = ☐   6 + 5 = ☐

10 7 + 7 = ☐   7 + 8 = ☐   6 + 7 = ☐

Name_____

Date_____

Set A

Add ☐

1   4 ⟶ ☐

2   7 ⟶ ☐

3   10 ⟶ ☐

4   8 ⟶ ☐

5   12 ⟶ ☐

Set B

Add ☐

1   5 ⟶ ☐

2   8 ⟶ ☐

3   11 ⟶ ☐

4   9 ⟶ ☐

5   6 ⟶ ☐

Set C

Add ☐

1   13 ⟶ ☐

2   10 ⟶ ☐

3   8 ⟶ ☐

4   11 ⟶ ☐

5   9 ⟶ ☐

Set D

Add ☐

1   12 ⟶ ☐

2   7 ⟶ ☐

3   11 ⟶ ☐

4   6 ⟶ ☐

5   8 ⟶ ☐

Name _____

Date _____

How many? Answer in words

1 Four more than eleven _____

2 Add six and twelve _____

3 Seven added to eight _____

4 Five plus nine _____

5 Ten more than three _____

6 Add nine and eleven _____

7 Five added to fourteen _____

8 Seven plus twelve _____

9 Eight more than nine _____

10 Fourteen plus six _____

Name

Date

Write sums that make 18

1 [ ] + [ ] = 18   **5** [ ] + [ ] = 18

2 [ ] + [ ] = 18   **6** [ ] + [ ] = 18

3 [ ] + [ ] = 18   **7** [ ] + [ ] = 18

4 [ ] + [ ] = 18   **8** [ ] + [ ] = 18

Write sums that make 19

1 [ ] + [ ] = 19   **5** [ ] + [ ] = 19

2 [ ] + [ ] = 19   **6** [ ] + [ ] = 19

3 [ ] + [ ] = 19   **7** [ ] + [ ] = 19

4 [ ] + [ ] = 19   **8** [ ] + [ ] = 19

Name _____

Date _____

Join the sums to their answers

2 + 10

10 + 1

9 + 3

2 + 9

1 + 10

3 + 9

10 + 4

3 + 10

4 + 9

9 + 5

4 + 10

5 + 10

6 + 9

5 + 9

6 + 10

7 + 9

10 + 5

9 + 6

10 + 6   10 + 7

9 + 7   8 + 9

7 + 10

9 + 9

8 + 10   9 + 10

9 + 8

10 + 8

9 + 10

10 + 9

10 + 10

10 + 9

| 11 |
| 12 |
| 13 |
| 14 |
| 15 |
| 16 |
| 17 |
| 18 |
| 19 |
| 20 |

Name_____

Date_____

How many altogether?

1   6 cars in a car park   7 more arrive   ☐ cars

2   12 people at a party   8 more arrive   ☐ people

3   Buy 7 sweets   Buy 9 more   ☐ sweets

4   10 flowers   Pick 8 more   ☐ flowers

5   Pour 5 drinks   Pour 8 more   ☐ drinks

6   Stick up 9 posters   Stick up 5 more   ☐ posters

7   Get 7 birthday cards   Get 12 more   ☐ cards

8   Post 8 letters   Post 9 more   ☐ letters

9   Buy 12 stickers   Buy 6 more   ☐ stickers

10   Light 14 candles   Light 6 more   ☐ candles

Name

Date

Fill in the missing numbers

1

5	4		2	1	0

2

6	5		3		1

3

9	8		6		

4

7	6			3	

5

5		3	2		

6

10	9		7		

7

8	7			4	

8

10		8	7		

Ring the sums that make 2

3 – 2   4 – 1   2 – 1

5 – 2   4 – 2

3 – 1   5 – 3   4 – 3

Ring the sums that make 3

4 – 2   5 – 1   3 – 0

4 – 1   5 – 2

2 – 1   4 – 3   5 – 3

Name

Date

How many? What is 1 less?

1 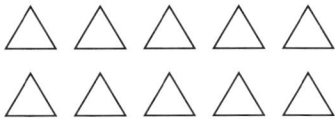 [ ]   1 less = [ ]

2 [ ]   1 less = [ ]

3 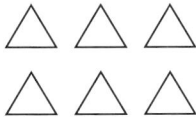 [ ]   1 less = [ ]

4 [ ]   1 less = [ ]

5 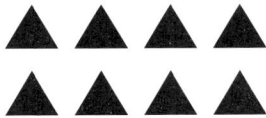 [ ]   1 less = [ ]

6 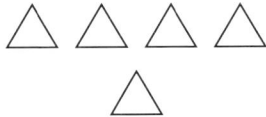 [ ]   1 less = [ ]

7 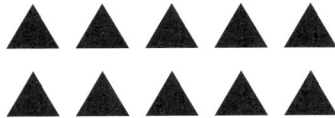 [ ]   1 less = [ ]

8 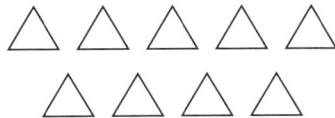 [ ]   1 less = [ ]

9  [ ]   1 less = [ ]

10 [ ]   1 less = [ ]

What is the difference between the two numbers?

1

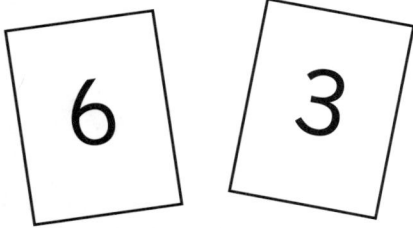

difference = ☐

5

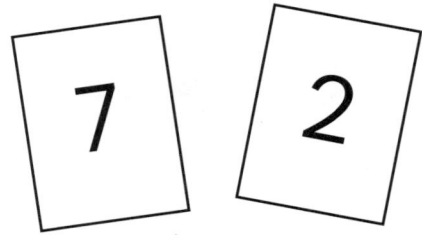

difference = ☐

2

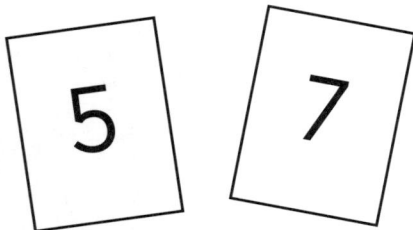

difference = ☐

6

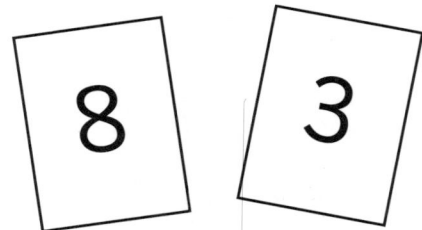

difference = ☐

3

difference = ☐

7

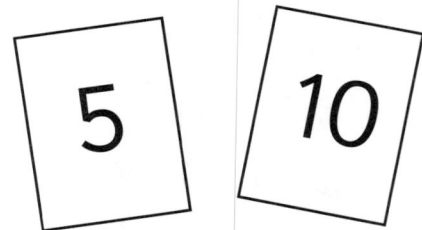

difference = ☐

4

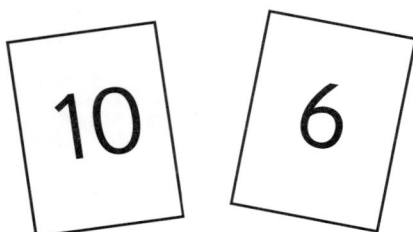

difference = ☐

8

difference = ☐

Name _____

Date _____

How many circles? Take away 3 from each set. How many left?

Set A	Set B	Set C

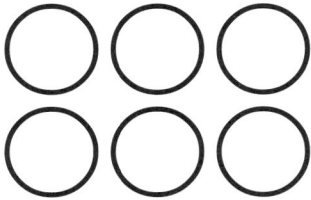 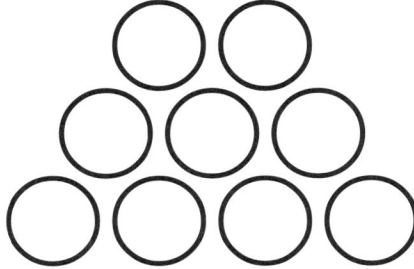 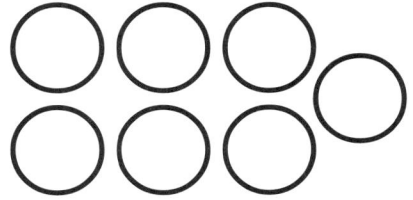

☐ − 3 = ☐   ☐ − 3 = ☐   ☐ − 3 = ☐

Set D	Set E	Set F

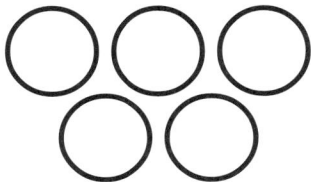 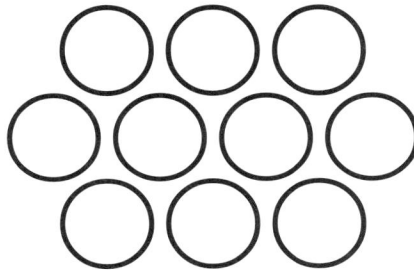 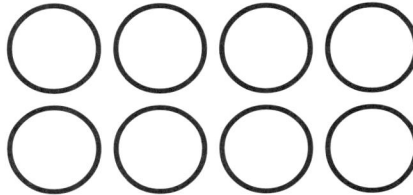

☐ − 3 = ☐   ☐ − 3 = ☐   ☐ − 3 = ☐

How many circles? Take away 4 from each set. How many left?

Set G	Set H	Set I

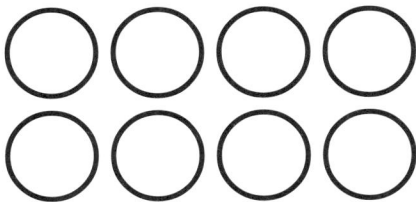 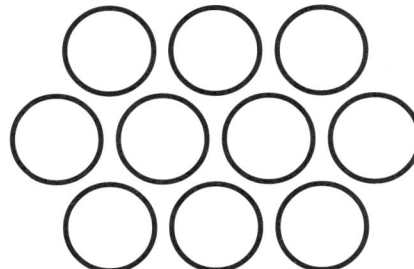 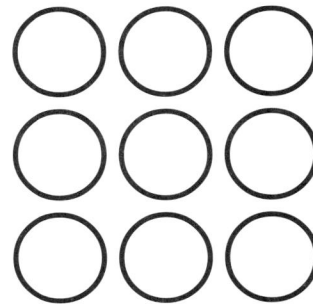

☐ − 4 = ☐   ☐ − 4 = ☐   ☐ − 4 = ☐

Name

Date

How many circles? Cross out to make each set equal 5

Set A ○○○○ ○○○

$\Box - \Box = 5$

Set B ○○○○○ ○○○○

$\Box - \Box = 5$

Set C ○○○ ○○○

$\Box - \Box = 5$

Set D ○○○○ ○○○○

$\Box - \Box = 5$

Set E ○○○○○ ○○○○

$\Box - \Box = 5$

Set F ○○○ ○○○○

$\Box - \Box = 5$

Now do these

Set G ○○○○○ ○○○○○

$\Box - \Box = 6$

Set H ○○○○○ ○○○○○

$\Box - \Box = 3$

Set I ○○○○○ ○○○○○

$\Box - \Box = 4$

Set J ○○○○○ ○○○○○

$\Box - \Box = 7$

Name _____

Date _____

Work out these as quickly as you can

Set A

1 6 − 4 = ☐

2 6 − 2 = ☐

3 6 − 5 = ☐

4 6 − 3 = ☐

Set B

1 7 − 2 = ☐

2 7 − 4 = ☐

3 7 − 5 = ☐

4 7 − 3 = ☐

Set C

1 8 − 2 = ☐

2 8 − 5 = ☐

3 8 − 3 = ☐

4 8 − 4 = ☐

5 8 − 6 = ☐

Set D

1 9 − 3 = ☐

2 9 − 5 = ☐

3 9 − 7 = ☐

4 9 − 4 = ☐

5 9 − 6 = ☐

Set E

1 10 − 4 = ☐

2 10 − 7 = ☐

3 10 − 2 = ☐

4 10 − 5 = ☐

5 10 − 6 = ☐

6 10 − 3 = ☐

Name_____

Date_____

Tick the correct sums. Cross the wrong ones. Write the correct

answer for the wrong ones ✓ or ✗

1   Seven take away three equals four ☐ _____

2   Ten subtract two equals eight ☐ _____

3   Nine minus five equals three ☐ _____

4   Eight take away four equals four ☐ _____

5   Seven subtract five equals two ☐ _____

6   Nine take away three equals six ☐ _____

7   Ten minus four equals five ☐ _____

8   Ten take away three equals seven ☐ _____

9   Eight minus five equals two ☐ _____

10 Ten take away six equals four ☐ _____

Name

Date

Use doubles to work out the sums in column 1. Then use your answer to column 1 to help you with column 2

1 $16 - 8 =$ ☐ $16 - 9 =$ ☐

2 $12 - 6 =$ ☐ $12 - 5 =$ ☐

3 $18 - 9 =$ ☐ $18 - 8 =$ ☐

4 $20 - 10 =$ ☐ $20 - 9 =$ ☐

5 $14 - 7 =$ ☐ $14 - 8 =$ ☐

6 $16 - 8 =$ ☐ $16 - 7 =$ ☐

7 $12 - 6 =$ ☐ $12 - 7 =$ ☐

8 $14 - 7 =$ ☐ $14 - 6 =$ ☐

9 $16 - 8 =$ ☐ $17 - 8 =$ ☐

10 $14 - 7 =$ ☐ $15 - 7 =$ ☐

Name_____

Date_____

Pick numbers from the box to complete the sums. You can use them more than once

Set A

| 17 | 3 |
| 7 | 13 |

20 – ☐ = ☐   10 – ☐ = ☐

20 – ☐ = ☐   10 – ☐ = ☐

Set B

| 4 | 14 |
| 16 | 6 |

20 – ☐ = ☐   10 – ☐ = ☐

20 – ☐ = ☐   10 – ☐ = ☐

Set C

| 12 | 8 |
| 2 | 18 |

20 – ☐ = ☐   10 – ☐ = ☐

20 – ☐ = ☐   10 – ☐ = ☐

Set D

| 9 | 11 |
| 1 | 19 |

20 – ☐ = ☐   10 – ☐ = ☐

20 – ☐ = ☐   10 – ☐ = ☐

Name _____

Date _____

Tick the pairs with a difference of 7 ✔

15	8	☐

16	7	☐

14	7	☐

12	5	☐

4	13	☐

6	11	☐

6	13	☐

8	16	☐

11	4	☐

Tick the pairs with a difference of 8 ✔

19	11	☐

6	14	☐

3	12	☐

15	7	☐

9	16	☐

17	9	☐

16	8	☐

11	3	☐

4	12	☐

Name _____

Date _____

Write the sum and work it out. How many left?

1 12 fish 8 swim away ☐ − ☐ = ☐

2 14 sweets Eat 5 ☐ − ☐ = ☐

3 18 letters Post 9 ☐ − ☐ = ☐

4 16 drinks Drink 7 ☐ − ☐ = ☐

5 17 birds 9 fly away ☐ − ☐ = ☐

6 20 ants 14 crawl away ☐ − ☐ = ☐

7 19 cakes Eat 12 ☐ − ☐ = ☐

8 18 butterflies 11 fly away ☐ − ☐ = ☐

9 15 lollies 7 melt ☐ − ☐ = ☐

10 20 rabbits 12 hop away ☐ − ☐ = ☐

Name

Date

Colour all the 1p coins

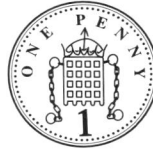

Put a ring around each of the 2p coins

Name _____

Date _____

Colour all the 5p coins

Put a cross on each 10p coin

Name

Date

Colour coins to make up 5p

| 1 1 1 / 1 1 1 | 5p | 1 2 / 2 1 | 5p |
| 2 1 1 / 1 1 | 5p | 5 1 / 1 2 | 5p |

Colour coins to make the amount shown

| 2 1 1 / 1 5 | 4p | 2 1 1 / 1 5 | 6p |
| 1 1 1 / 2 1 1 | 6p | 1 2 / 2 5 | 4p |

Name_____

Date_____

Draw the coins to make each amount

7p	
5p	
9p	
6p	
4p	
8p	
10p	
10p	Do this a different way

Draw a ring around sums that make 10p

4p + 6p   3p + 5p   5p + 4p

            7p + 3p   9p + 1p

2p + 7p   6p + 4p   8p + 2p

            3p + 6p   5p + 5p

Draw a ring around sums that make 9p

4p + 6p   3p + 5p   5p + 4p

            7p + 3p   9p + 1p

2p + 7p   6p + 4p   8p + 2p

            3p + 6p   5p + 5p

Fill in the gaps

1   Spend 4p   Change from 5p is [   ] p

2   Spend 2p   Change from 5p is [   ] p

3   Spend 3p   Change from 5p is [   ] p

How much change from 10p each time?

1   Spend 2p   Change is [   ] p   6   Spend 8p   Change is [   ] p

2   Spend 5p   Change is [   ] p   7   Spend 6p   Change is [   ] p

3   Spend 7p   Change is [   ] p   8   Spend 4p   Change is [   ] p

4   Spend 10p Change is [   ] p   9   Spend 9p   Change is [   ] p

5   Spend 1p   Change is [   ] p   10   Spend 3p   Change is [   ] p

Name

Date

 2p 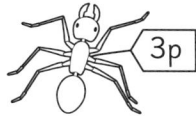 3p 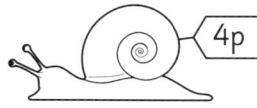 4p 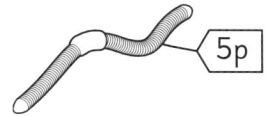 5p

How much?

1 and ☐ p + ☐ p = ☐ p

2 and ☐ p + ☐ p = ☐ p

3 and ☐ p + ☐ p = ☐ p

4 and ☐ p + ☐ p = ☐ p

5 and ☐ p + ☐ p = ☐ p

6 and ☐ p + ☐ p = ☐ p

7 and and ☐ p + ☐ p + ☐ p = ☐ p

2p   3p   4p   5p

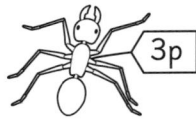

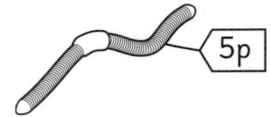

How much change from 10p?

1   + = [ ]p   Change = [ ]p

2   + = [ ]p   Change = [ ]p

3   + = [ ]p   Change = [ ]p

4   + = [ ]p   Change = [ ]p

5   + + = [ ]p   Change = [ ]p

6   + + = [ ]p   Change = [ ]p

7   + + = [ ]p   Change = [ ]p

What is the largest value coin you can use to start making these amounts? How much more is needed?

1 To make 9p use a ☐ p coin   Need ☐ p more

2 To make 13p use a ☐ p coin   Need ☐ p more

3 To make 17p use a ☐ p coin   Need ☐ p more

4 To make 25p use a ☐ p coin   Need ☐ p more

5 To make 21p use a ☐ p coin   Need ☐ p more

6 To make 19p use a ☐ p coin   Need ☐ p more

7 To make 34p use a ☐ p coin   Need ☐ p more

8 To make 27p use a ☐ p coin   Need ☐ p more

9 To make 15p use a ☐ p coin   Need ☐ p more

10 To make 31p use a ☐ p coin   Need ☐ p more

Name _____

Date _____

Draw one more coin in each set to make the amount shown

Set A

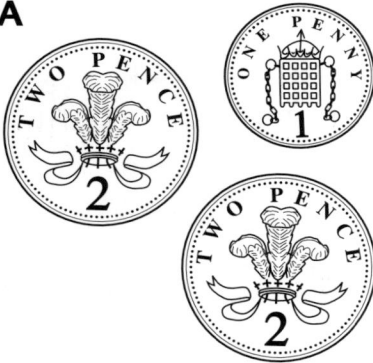

7p

Set B

11p

Set C

14p

Set D

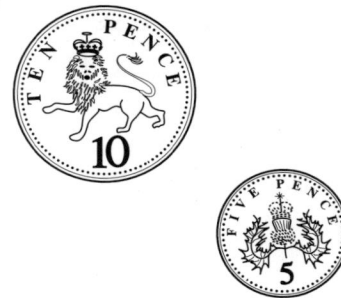

17p

Set E

15p

Set F

19p

Set G

16p

Set H

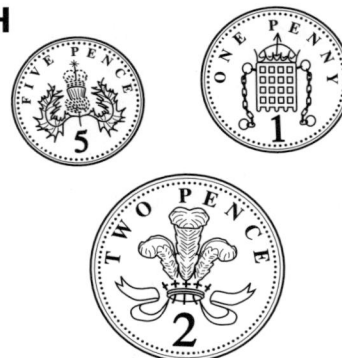

18p

Name _____

Date _____

Set A

☐☐

1	4	⟶	☐ p
2	7	⟶	☐ p
3	12	⟶	☐ p
4	5	⟶	☐ p
5	11	⟶	☐ p

Set B

☐☐

1	3	⟶	☐ p
2	9	⟶	☐ p
3	14	⟶	☐ p
4	8	⟶	☐ p
5	6	⟶	☐ p

Set C

☐☐

1	5	⟶	☐ p
2	9	⟶	☐ p
3	4	⟶	☐ p
4	10	⟶	☐ p
5	7	⟶	☐ p

Set D

☐☐

1	8	⟶	☐ p
2	6	⟶	☐ p
3	10	⟶	☐ p
4	3	⟶	☐ p
5	9	⟶	☐ p

Fill in the missing amounts

1   7p + [p] = 12p

2   5p + [p] = 11p

3   9p + [p] = 13p

4   8p + [p] = 11p

5   6p + [p] = 13p

6   4p + [p] = 12p

7   7p + [p] = 15p

8   8p + [p] = 13p

9   9p + [p] = 15p

10   5p + [p] = 14p

11   [p] + 6p = 12p

12   [p] + 8p = 16p

13   [p] + 7p = 13p

14   [p] + 9p = 17p

15   [p] + 4p = 16p

16   [p] + 6p = 14p

17   [p] + 8p = 19p

18   [p] + 7p = 16p

19   [p] + 9p = 18p

20   [p] + 6p = 15p

Name

Date

Tick the sums that make 20p   ✔ or ✘

Cross the sums that do not make 20p

1	5p + 15p	☐	11	13p + 7p	☐
2	7p + 14p	☐	12	16p + 4p	☐
3	8p + 12p	☐	13	11p + 9p	☐
4	4p + 15p	☐	14	8p + 13p	☐
5	6p + 14p	☐	15	4p + 17p	☐
6	10p + 10p	☐	16	15p + 6p	☐
7	16p + 5p	☐	17	18p + 2p	☐
8	7p + 13p	☐	18	11p + 11p	☐
9	15p + 4p	☐	19	3p + 17p	☐
10	12p + 7p	☐	20	15p + 5p	☐

Name_____

Date_____

How much change from 15p?

1   Spend 11p Change is [   ] p   **3**   Spend 13p Change is [   ] p

2   Spend 14p Change is [   ] p   **4**   Spend 12p Change is [   ] p

How much change from 20p?

1   Spend 5p   Change is [   ] p   **7**   Spend 13p Change is [   ] p

2   Spend 14p Change is [   ] p   **8**   Spend 8p   Change is [   ] p

3   Spend 10p Change is [   ] p   **9**   Spend 12p Change is [   ] p

4   Spend 18p Change is [   ] p   **10** Spend 16p Change is [   ] p

5   Spend 9p   Change is [   ] p   **11** Spend 7p   Change is [   ] p

6   Spend 15p Change is [   ] p   **12** Spend 11p Change is [   ] p

1 Bob has 20p and he spends 13p. How much has he left?

[ ] p

2 Sarah has 16p made up of three coins. What are they?

___

3 How much do three 5p coins make? [ ] p

4 Jack has two 5p coins and four 2p coins.

How much is that? [ ] p

5 Kelly buys a chew for 8p and a biscuit for 12p.

How much does she spend? [ ] p

6 Which three coins make 13p? ___

7 Rachel wants to buy a pencil for 19p. She has 8p.

How much more does she need? [ ] p

8 Gary has a 5p coin and six 2p coins. How much

is that? [ ] p

Ring the correct middle day

1	Monday	Tuesday Friday	Wednesday
2	Thursday	Friday Wednesday	Saturday
3	Tuesday	Wednesday Monday	Thursday
4	Friday	Saturday Monday	Sunday

What day is next? Ring the correct one

5	**Tuesday:**	Wednesday	Monday	Thursday
6	**Monday:**	Thursday	Sunday	Tuesday
7	**Friday:**	Saturday	Monday	Thursday
8	**Wednesday:**	Thursday	Tuesday	Friday
9	**Saturday:**	Monday	Sunday	Friday
10	**Thursday:**	Friday	Saturday	Wednesday

Name

Date

What time is it?

1
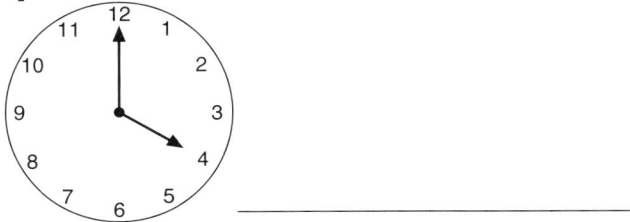
_____

2
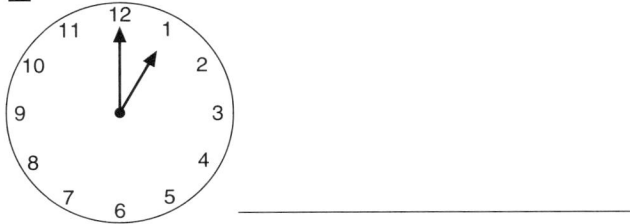
_____

3
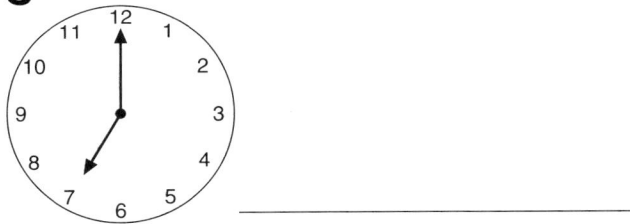
_____

4
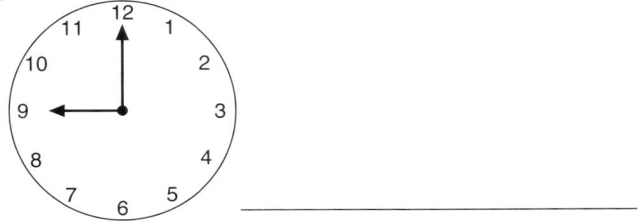
_____

5
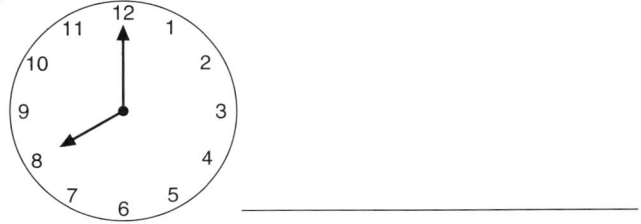
_____

6
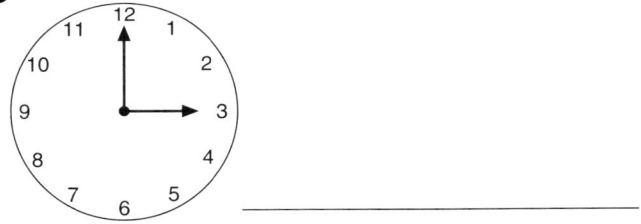
_____

Show the times on the clocks

7

2 o'clock
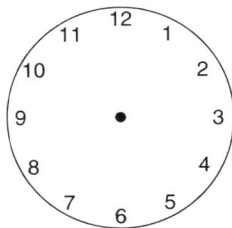

8

10 o'clock
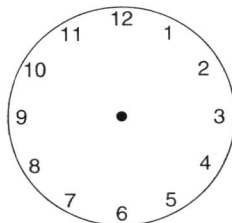

9

6 o'clock
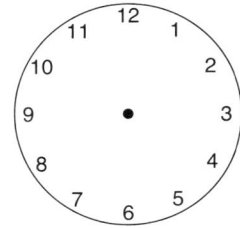

10

11 o'clock
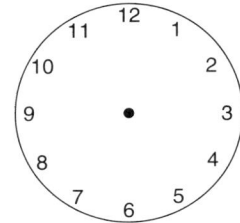

Name_____

Date_____

Make pairs of clocks tell the same time

1  [   ]   **5** 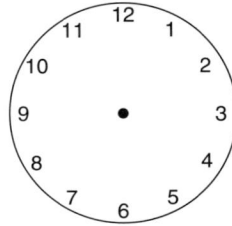 5:00

2  [   ]   **6** 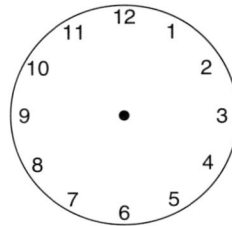 8:00

3 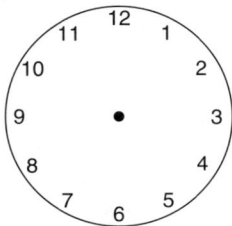 10:00   **7**  [   ]

4  [   ]   **8** 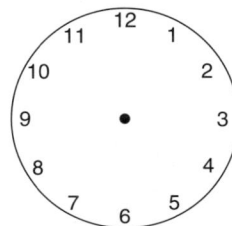 6:00

Name _____

Date _____

Fill in the days

	Today	Yesterday	Day after tomorrow
1	Monday	_____	_____
2	Thursday	_____	_____
3	Sunday	_____	_____
4	Friday	_____	_____
5	_____	Monday	_____
6	_____	_____	Monday
7	_____	Tuesday	_____
8	_____	_____	Wednesday
9	_____	Thursday	_____

Name_____

Date_____

Join the months in order

July

January

May

June

February

August

April

September

November

March

October

December

What month comes next?

1 March _____   **4** May _____

2 August _____   **5** October _____

3 November _____   **6** January _____

72

Name

Date

What time is it?

1 6:15 _____
_____

2 10:30 _____
_____

3 4:45 _____
_____

4 7:00 _____
_____

5 3:15 _____
_____

6 2:45 _____
_____

7 _____
_____

8 _____
_____

9 _____
_____

10 _____
_____

11 _____
_____

12 _____
_____

Make both clocks show the given time

1   5 o'clock   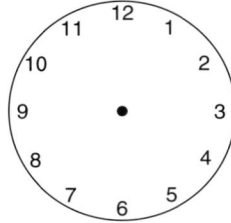   5:00

2   Half past 7

3   Quarter past 2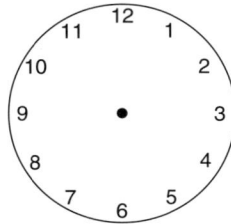

4   Half past 9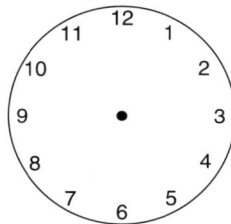

5   Quarter past 6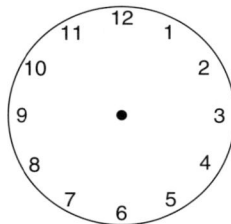

6   Quarter to 8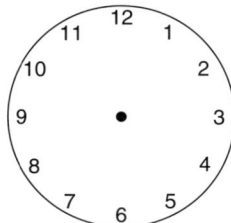

7   Quarter to 3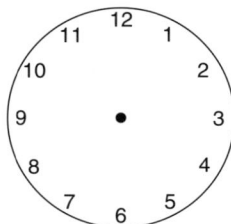

Name _____

Date _____

Join times that are equal

15 minutes   1 hour   2 hours

        30 minutes $\frac{1}{4}$ hour

120 minutes $\frac{3}{4}$ hour   60 minutes

        $\frac{1}{2}$ hour   45 minutes

Complete these

1 1 hour = ☐ minutes   **4** 120 minutes = ☐ hours

2 $\frac{1}{2}$ hour = ☐ minutes   **5** 45 minutes = ☐ hour

3 $\frac{1}{4}$ hour = ☐ minutes   **6** 30 minutes = ☐ hour

How long is it from one time to the other?

1   From 4 o'clock to 5 o'clock?   _____

2   From 2:30 to 3:30?   _____

3   From half past ten to
       half past eleven?   _____

4   From 4:15 to 6:15?   _____

5   From 1:30 to 2:00?   _____

6   From 9:00 to 9:30?   _____

7   From 2 o'clock to 2:15?   _____

8   From ten o'clock to
       quarter to eleven?   _____

9   From 12:15 to 1:00?   _____

10 From 8:45 to 9:15?   _____

Name _____

Date _____

Draw the new times

1

15 minutes later

2

$\frac{1}{4}$ hour earlier

3

15 minutes later

4

$\frac{1}{2}$ hour earlier

5

$\frac{1}{2}$ hour later

6

$\frac{1}{2}$ hour earlier

7

30 minutes later

8

$\frac{3}{4}$ hour later

Associated Topics

Fractions ▷

Pattern ▷

Shape and Space ▷

Fractions

LEVEL 1

Learning Objectives

To be able to:
1. Recognize and find half of a whole one

1 RECOGNIZE AND FIND HALF OF A WHOLE ONE

C65-66

Ideas for whole class work

Have some paper shapes at the front. Choose a child to come out and fold one of the shapes in half. Note that there are two parts and that they are equal. Do this for several shapes. Then introduce some shapes that can not be folded in half. Hold up a shape and ask if it can be folded in half. Choose a child to come out and check.

Copymasters
C65 Fractions *Find half*

C66 Fractions *Find half*

LEVEL 2

Learning Objectives

To be able to:
1. Recognize and find quarter of a whole one
2. Find half or quarter of a set of objects
3. Use halves and quarters

1 RECOGNIZE AND FIND QUARTER OF A WHOLE ONE

C67

Ideas for whole class work

Have some paper shapes at the front and choose a child to come out and fold a shape into quarters. Note that there are four parts and that they are equal. Do this for several shapes. Then introduce some shapes that can not be folded into quarters. Hold up a shape and ask if it can be folded into quarters. Choose a child to come out and check.

Copymasters
C67 Fractions *Find quarter*

2 FIND HALF OR QUARTER OF A SET OF OBJECTS

C68-70

Ideas for whole class work

1 Have six children at the front and ask how many would be in each group if the six were split into two equal groups. Check by moving the children into two groups. Ask what fraction of the whole group is one of the small groups. Write half on the board and emphasize the two equal groups. Do this with other groups of children and do the same with cubes and other resources.

2 It is important when finding quarters that children think of it as four equal groups and not half and then half again. If they begin to form the link between the denominator and the number of groups at this stage it helps them to understand how fractions work later on. Have four children at the front. Have 12 cubes in your hand and tell the children that you are going to share the cubes out equally so that there are four equal groups or quarters. Ask how many they will have each and share them out to check. Do this for other numbers of cubes, probably up to about 20 to start with.

3 Have the children in small groups with access to cubes such as Multilink®. Ask them to make a rod, with half the cubes blue. Do not state a size. Now ask them to make a different rod, half of which is blue. Compare the rods that different groups make and write the size of the rods on the board. Note that the sizes go up in twos and that they are all even numbers. Next move on to making rods with a quarter blue. You may need to give a size. For example, make a rod eight cubes long with a quarter of the cubes blue. Some children may be ready to note the numbers which work and the numbers which do not.

Copymasters
C68 Fractions *Find half of a set*

C69 Fractions *Find half or quarter*

C70 Fractions *Find half or quarter*

3 USE HALVES AND QUARTERS

C71

Ideas for whole class work
Show the children four cubes in one hand. Tell them that they are half the cubes you have got and that the other half of the cubes are in your other hand. Ask how many cubes are in your other hand and how many you have altogether. Do this for other numbers of cubes. Next, try showing them quarter of the cubes and ask how many there are altogether.

Copymasters
C71 Fractions *Use halves and quarters*

Pattern

LEVEL **1**	**Learning Objectives**

Learning Objectives

To be able to:
1. Recognize and continue patterns

2. Count repeats in patterns

---

1 RECOGNIZE AND CONTINUE PATTERNS

C72

Ideas for whole class work
Have some coloured shapes at the front. You may wish to restrict the choice at first. Choose two children to come out and select two shapes. Either Blu-Tak® them to the board or let the children hold them up. Tell the children that these are the first two shapes in a repeating pattern. Add the next two shapes yourself so that they can see the pattern beginning to repeat and ask a child to come out and select the next shape in the pattern. Continue the pattern for a few repeats. Do this for lots of other patterns. Next, move on to repeating three shapes.

Copymasters
C72 Pattern *Recognize and continue patterns*

2 COUNT REPEATS IN PATTERNS

C73

Ideas for whole class work
Set up repeating patterns as in Learning Objective 1 and ask questions. How many triangles are there? What is the repeating pattern? How many shapes are in each repeat? How many times does the pattern repeat? And so on.

Copymasters
C73 Pattern *Count repeats*

LEVEL **2**	**Learning Objectives**

Learning Objectives

To be able to:
1. Identify odd and even numbers

2. Continue sequences of numbers
3. Count in steps of 2, 3, 5 and 10

---

1 IDENTIFY ODD AND EVEN NUMBERS

C74

Ideas for whole class work
1 Draw a number line on the board from 1 to 20. Put some cube rods in a bag for a selection of odd and even numbers from 1 to 20. Show the children how to check for even numbers by putting the cubes in twos; if there is one left over, it is an odd number. Get a child to come and pick a rod of cubes from the bag. They then count the cubes and work out whether the number is odd or even. They colour their number on the number line, for example, red for even numbers and blue for odd numbers. Do this for several numbers. Discuss the pattern that emerges and predict what colour other numbers will be. You may wish to extend the pattern on a 1–100 grid.

2 Give clues for children to identify numbers using odd and even in your clues. For example: I am thinking of a number less than 20 but more than 17; it is an odd number; what is it?

Copymasters
C74 Pattern *Odds and evens*

2 | CONTINUE SEQUENCES OF NUMBERS
C75

Ideas for whole class work
Start by using a number line to 20 and extend this on to a 1–100 grid. Colour a sequence of numbers and choose a child to come and colour the next number and another child to colour the next. Ask how they know which one to colour. Get the children to count the sequence out loud and possibly to continue it even further. You may wish to use coloured squares and Blu-Tak® instead of colouring the numbers. Next, ask a child to come and set up a sequence for the other children to continue.

Copymasters
C75 Pattern *Continue sequences*

3 | COUNT IN STEPS OF 2, 3, 5 AND 10
C76-77

Ideas for whole class work
Verbally, give each child a number. Tell them the start number and the rule to follow. For example, start on 1 and keep adding 2. The children say their own number out loud as it is needed to make the sequence 1, 3, 5, 7, and so on. Choose other start numbers and rules. Give the children different numbers. Next, try starting with 30 and have a rule such as subtract 3. Try giving the children numbers starting from 20 or more instead of 1.

Copymasters
C76 Pattern *Count in steps: add*

C77 Pattern *Count in steps: subtract*

Shape and Space

LEVEL **1**

Learning Objectives

To be able to:
1. Describe positions

2. Sort 2D and 3D shapes

1 | DESCRIBE POSITIONS

Ideas for whole class work
1 Have at the front a small open box, such as a shoe box, and a small object. Put the object in different positions in relation to the box – for example, in it, on it, under it, behind it, and so on – and ask the children to describe where it is. Then reverse this and give the object to a child and ask them to put it in a particular position.

2 Choose a child and quietly ask them to put themselves, for example, on a chair, beside the table, behind the bookcase. Then ask the other children for a sentence describing where the first child is.

Copymasters
None.

2 | SORT 2D AND 3D SHAPES
C78

Ideas for whole class work
1 Have a variety of 2D shapes at the front. Give clues and ask a child to tell you which shape you are thinking of. When the children are competent at this, let one of them give the clues. Next, think of a shape and get the children to ask you questions about the shape to determine which one it is. Focus on the vocabulary of shape. Many children find it hard to ask questions like this. This can also be done with 3D shapes.

2 Have a variety of 2D shapes at the front. Select some and sort them into two sets. Get the children to work out the criteria for your sets. Hold up a new shape and ask into which set it should go and why. Do this for other shapes and sets. This can also be done with 3D shapes.

Copymasters
C78 Shape and Space *Sort shapes*

Learning Objectives

To be able to:
1. Name 2D and 3D shapes and use language of shape
2. Recognize right angles and know left and right

1 NAME 2D AND 3D SHAPES AND USE LANGUAGE OF SHAPE

C79-80

2 RECOGNIZE RIGHT ANGLES AND KNOW LEFT AND RIGHT

C81

Ideas for whole class work

1 Have a variety of shapes at the front. Make sure you include irregular shapes. Choose two children to come out and pick out, for example, all the triangles or all the four-sided shapes. Repeat this for other shapes such as pentagons and hexagons.

2 The children will need a pencil and paper. You need a card with a small design on it made up of shapes and lines, for example, a square with a small triangle inside it. You give instructions using appropriate vocabulary and the children have to try to draw your design.

3 Have a variety of 3D shapes at the front. Use packets and containers as well as mathematical solids. Sort the shapes in lots of different ways, counting the number of faces, shapes of faces, curved surfaces, edges, and so on. Give clues for the children to guess your shape. Get the children to ask questions to determine your shape. Put the solids in a feely bag and get the children to describe the shape they can feel for others to work out the name of it. Take it out of the bag to check.

Copymasters
C79 Shape and Space *2D shapes*

C80 Shape and Space *3D shapes*

Ideas for whole class work
Choose a child to stand up and give them instructions to walk a short route, for example, forward three steps, turn one right angle to the right, and so on. Give instructions for the children to take their pencil through a route on paper. Copymaster C81 provides two mazes to practise this.

Copymasters
C81 Shape and Space *Right angles/know left and right* Give instructions for the children to trace a route through the maze. Tell them where to start and see if they end at the right place.

Name

Date

Draw a line to make two halves

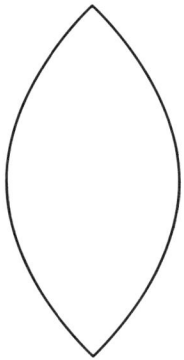

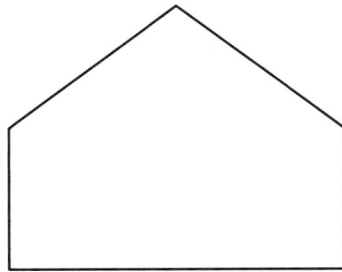

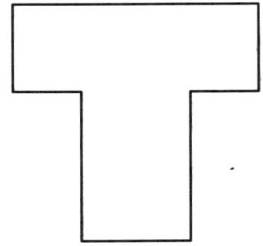

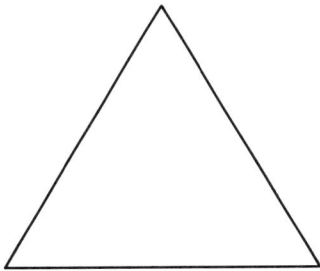

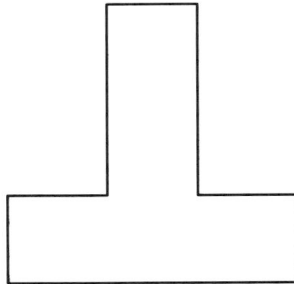

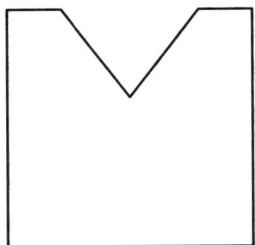

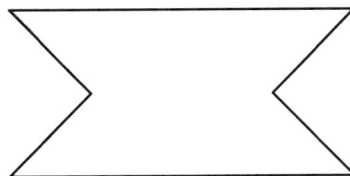

Draw the missing half

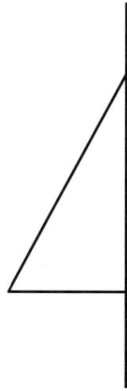

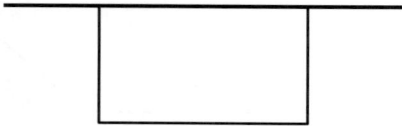

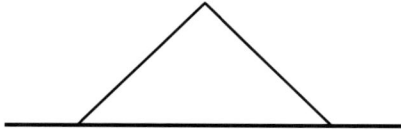

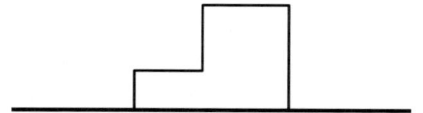

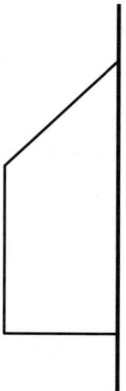

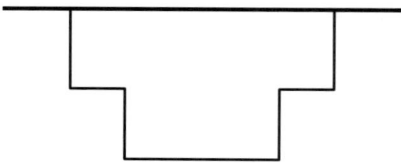

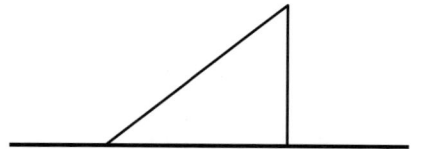

Name _____

Date _____

Shade a quarter

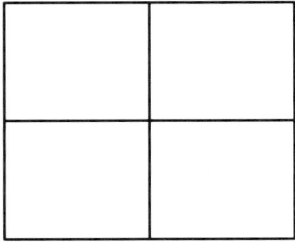

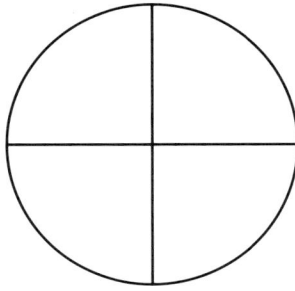

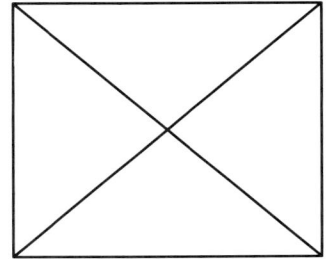

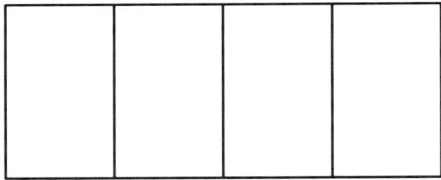

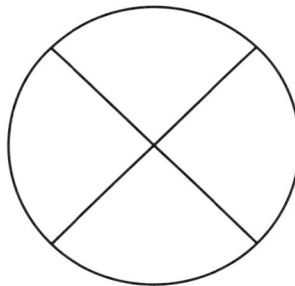

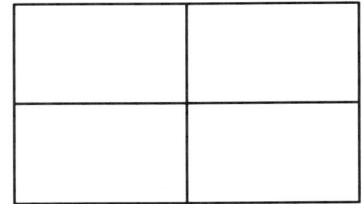

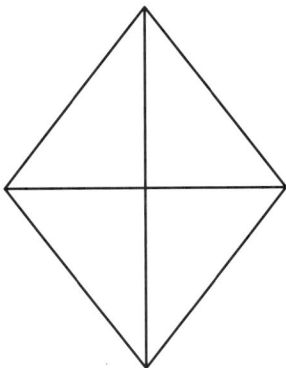

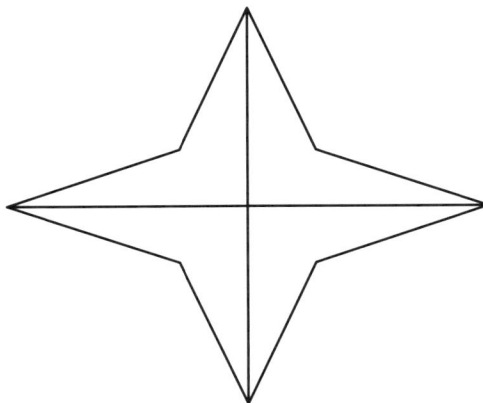

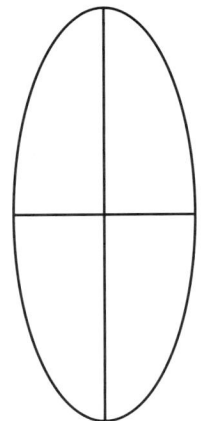

Name_____

Date_____

How many in the set? Find half

1 ○○○○○○ ☐ ½ of ☐ = ☐

2 ○○○○ ☐ ½ of ☐ = ☐

3 ○○○○○○
○○○○○○ ☐ ½ of ☐ = ☐

4 ○○○○○
○○○○○ ☐ ½ of ☐ = ☐

5 ○○○○○○
○○○○○○
○○○○○○ ☐ ½ of ☐ = ☐

6 ○○○○○
○○○○○
○○○○○ ☐ ½ of ☐ = ☐

7 ○○○○○○○○
○○○○○○○○ ☐ ½ of ☐ = ☐

8 ○○○○○
○○○○○
○○○○○
○○○○○ ☐ ½ of ☐ = ☐

Work these out

1 $\frac{1}{2}$ of 10 = ☐

2 $\frac{1}{2}$ of 4 = ☐

3 $\frac{1}{4}$ of 8 = ☐

4 $\frac{1}{2}$ of 14 = ☐

5 $\frac{1}{4}$ of 4 = ☐

6 $\frac{1}{2}$ of 6 = ☐

7 $\frac{1}{2}$ of 18 = ☐

8 $\frac{1}{2}$ of 12 = ☐

9 $\frac{1}{4}$ of 16 = ☐

10 $\frac{1}{2}$ of 20 = ☐

11 $\frac{1}{2}$ of 16 = ☐

12 $\frac{1}{4}$ of 12 = ☐

13 $\frac{1}{2}$ of 2 = ☐

14 $\frac{1}{4}$ of 20 = ☐

Now try these

1 $\frac{1}{2}$ of 24 = ☐

2 $\frac{1}{4}$ of 24 = ☐

3 $\frac{1}{2}$ of 22 = ☐

4 $\frac{1}{2}$ of 26 = ☐

Name _____

Date _____

Is the second number half of the first? ✔ or ✘

1	12 → 6	☐	**6**	20 → 10	☐
2	18 → 8	☐	**7**	14 → 7	☐
3	15 → 7	☐	**8**	6 → 4	☐
4	8 → 4	☐	**9**	10 → 5	☐
5	16 → 8	☐	**10**	13 → 6	☐

Is the second number a quarter of the first? ✔ or ✘

1	8 → 4	☐	**6**	12 → 3	☐
2	10 → 3	☐	**7**	20 → 5	☐
3	16 → 4	☐	**8**	8 → 2	☐
4	4 → 1	☐	**9**	18 → 4	☐
5	9 → 3	☐	**10**	20 → 10	☐

How many in the whole set if:

Set A

1 $\frac{1}{2}$ is 4   ☐

2 $\frac{1}{4}$ is 2   ☐

3 $\frac{1}{2}$ is 8   ☐

4 $\frac{1}{2}$ is 6   ☐

5 $\frac{1}{4}$ is 3   ☐

6 $\frac{1}{2}$ is 1   ☐

7 $\frac{1}{4}$ is 4   ☐

8 $\frac{1}{2}$ is 11   ☐

Set B

1 $\frac{1}{2}$ is 9   ☐

2 $\frac{1}{4}$ is 5   ☐

3 $\frac{1}{2}$ is 10   ☐

4 $\frac{1}{2}$ is 3   ☐

5 $\frac{1}{4}$ is 1   ☐

6 $\frac{1}{2}$ is 5   ☐

7 $\frac{1}{2}$ is 7   ☐

8 $\frac{1}{4}$ is 6   ☐

Name _____

Date _____

Ring the shape that comes next

1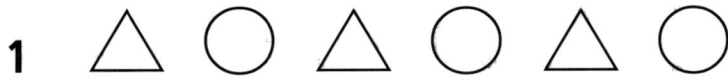

2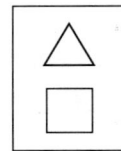

3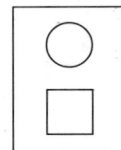

4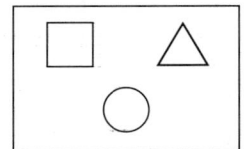

5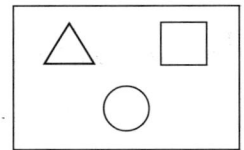

6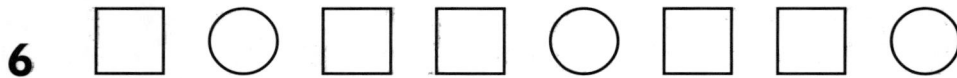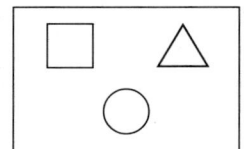

Draw the next two shapes

7  _____

8  _____

Name

Date

Ring the repeating pattern. How many times does the pattern appear?

1 ☐ ○ ☐ ○ ☐ ○ ☐ ○ | 4 | times

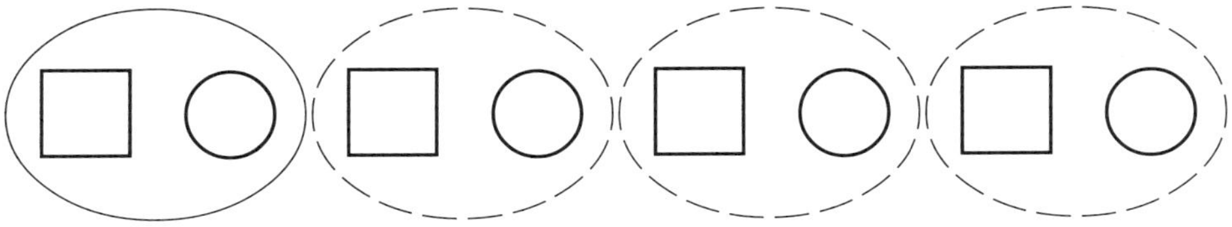

2 △ ☐ △ ☐ △ ☐ | | times

3 ○ △ ○ △ ○ △ ○ △ ○ △ ○ △ | | times

4 ☐ ☐ ○ ☐ ☐ ○ ☐ ☐ ○ | | times

5 ○ △ ☐ ○ △ ☐ | | times

6 △ ☐ ☐ △ ☐ ☐ △ ☐ ☐ | | times

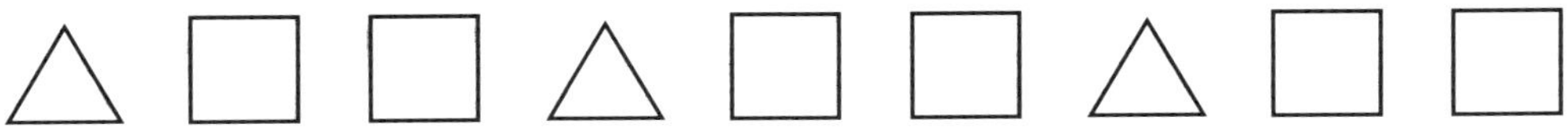

7 ○ ☐ ○ ☐ ○ ☐ ○ ☐ ○ ☐ | | times

8 △ ○ △ △ ○ △ △ ○ △ △ ○ △ | | times

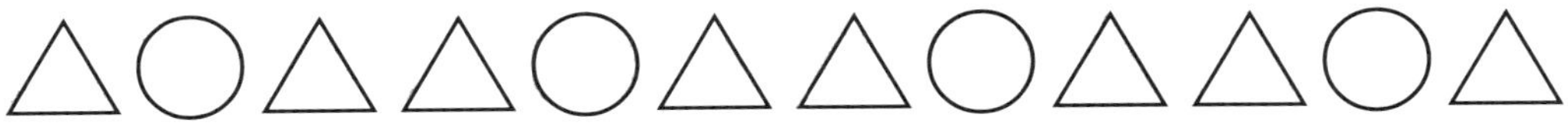

Name_____

Date_____

A Write these numbers in the correct set

1   4   12   3   6   15   18   10   7   19

even numbers

odd numbers

B Write these numbers in the correct set

24   31   65   72   81   39   76   94

even numbers

odd numbers

C Solve the puzzles

1 An odd number, less than 17, more than 14

2 An even number, less than 16, more than 13

3 An odd number, less than 25, more than 22

Name_____

Date_____

Write the two missing numbers

1   2   4   6   8   10   ▢   ▢

2   3   6   9   12   ▢   ▢   21

3   9   11   13   ▢   17   ▢   21

4   22   24   26   28   30   ▢   ▢

5   17   19   21   23   25   ▢   ▢

6   14   12   10   8   6   ▢   ▢

7   1   4   7   10   13   ▢   ▢

8   13   11   9   7   5   ▢   ▢

9   2   5   8   ▢   14   ▢   20

10   31   33   35   ▢   39   ▢   43

Name _____

Date _____

Follow the rule. Write the numbers

	Rule					
1	+3	Start on 1	4			
2	+2	Start on 7	9			
3	+3	Start on 8	11			
4	+5	Start on 5			20	
5	+2	Start on 12				
6	+5	Start on 13				
7	+10	Start on 4	14			
8	+3	Start on 12				
9	+10	Start on 26				
10	+5	Start on 21				

Follow the rule. Write the numbers

1 -2 ▷ Start on 20 | 18 | | | |

2 -10 ▷ Start on 50 | | | | |

3 -3 ▷ Start on 30 | | | | |

4 -5 ▷ Start on 30 | | | | |

5 -10 ▷ Start on 72 | | | | |

6 -2 ▷ Start on 39 | | | | |

7 -3 ▷ Start on 46 | | | | |

8 -10 ▷ Start on 61 | | | | |

9 -5 ▷ Start on 42 | | | | |

10 -10 ▷ Start on 87 | | | | |

Name_____

Date_____

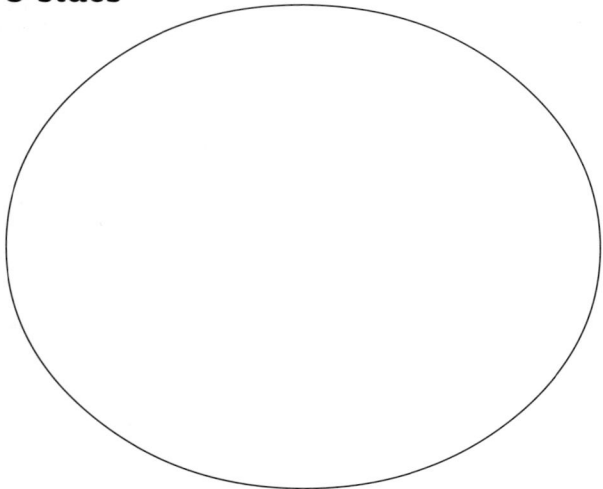

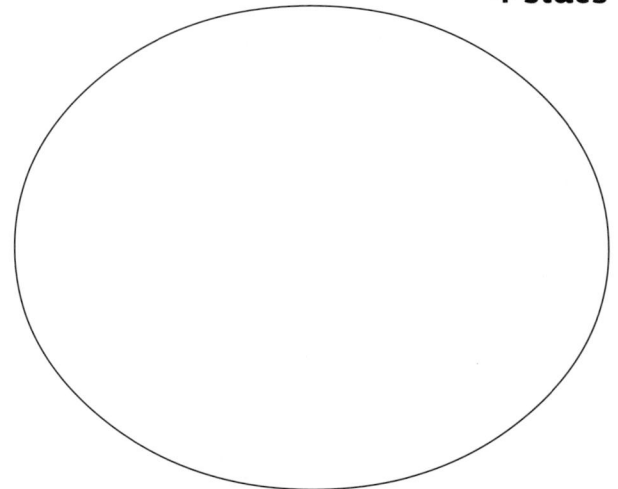

Put these shapes in the sets

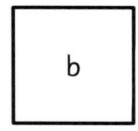

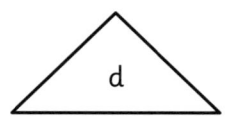

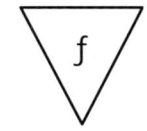

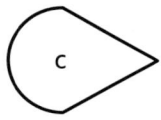

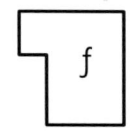

a   b   c   d   e   f   g

3 sides   **4 sides**

Put these shapes in the sets

a   b   c   d   e   f   g

all straight sides   **not all straight sides**

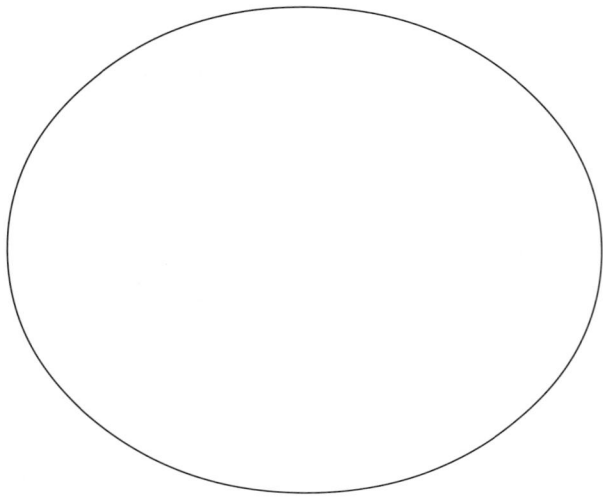

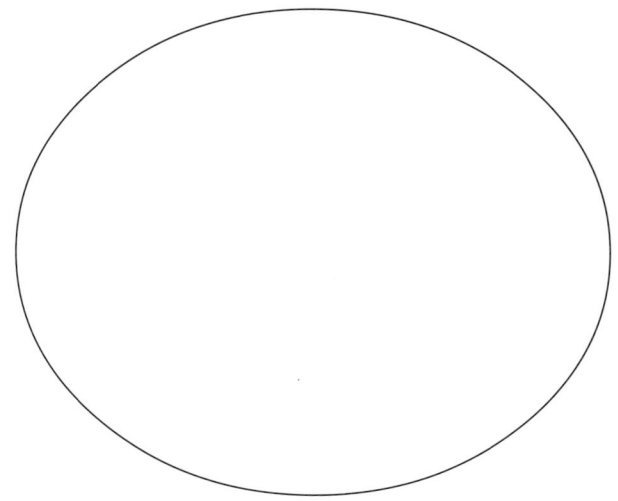

Name

Date

Put these shapes in the sets

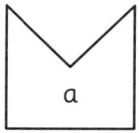 a
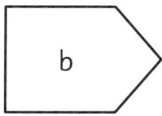 b
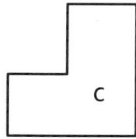 c
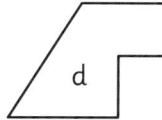 d
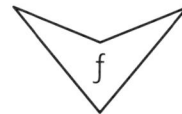 e
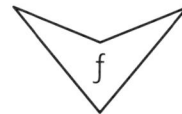 f
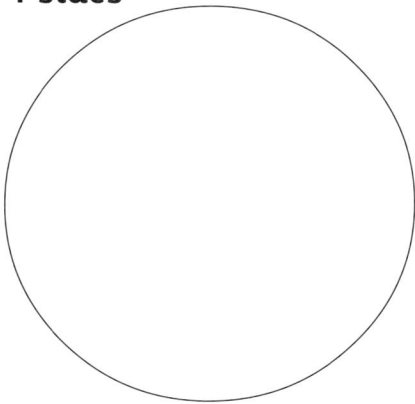 g

4 sides

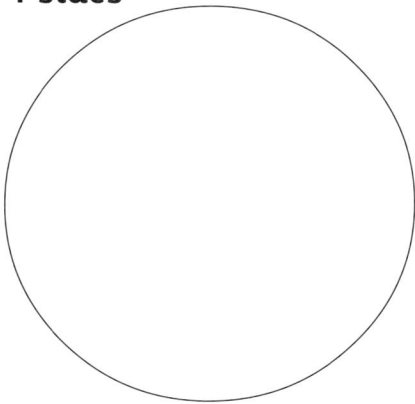

5 sides

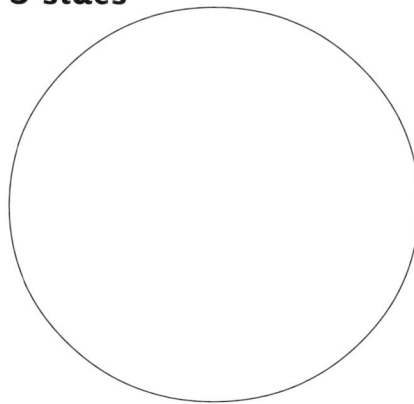

6 sides

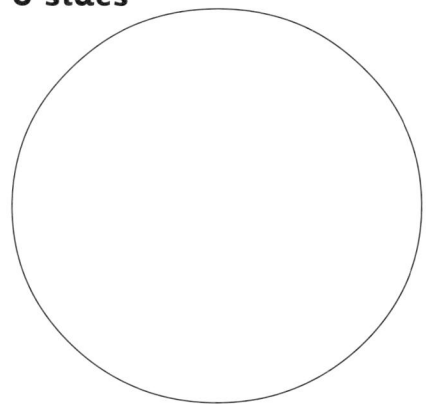

Name these shapes

1

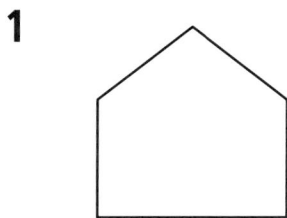

_____

2

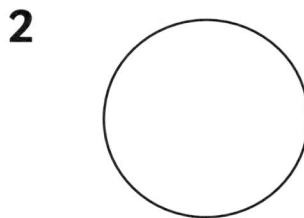

_____

3

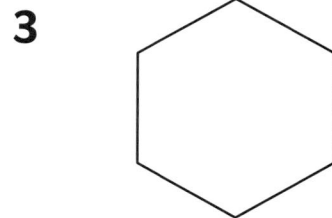

_____

4

_____

5

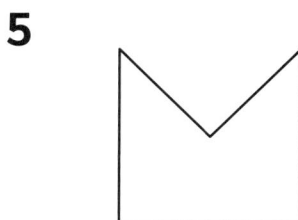

_____

6

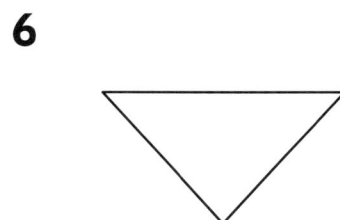

_____

Name

Date

Name these shapes

1

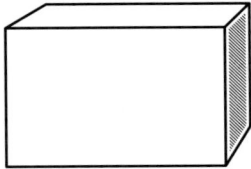

2

3

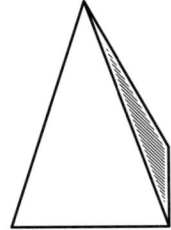

4

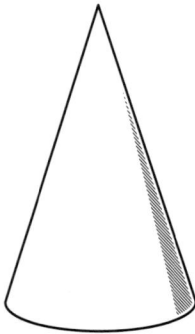

5

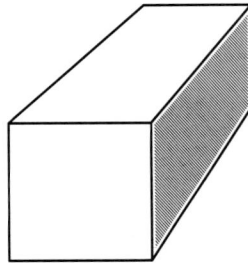

6

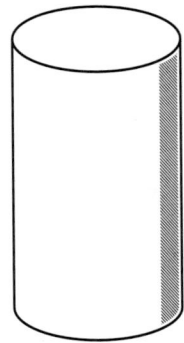

7

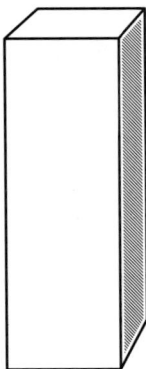

8

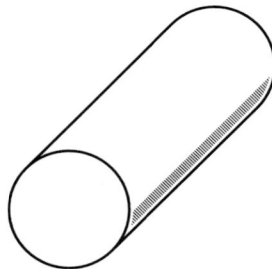

9

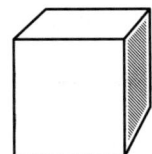

Travel along the lines

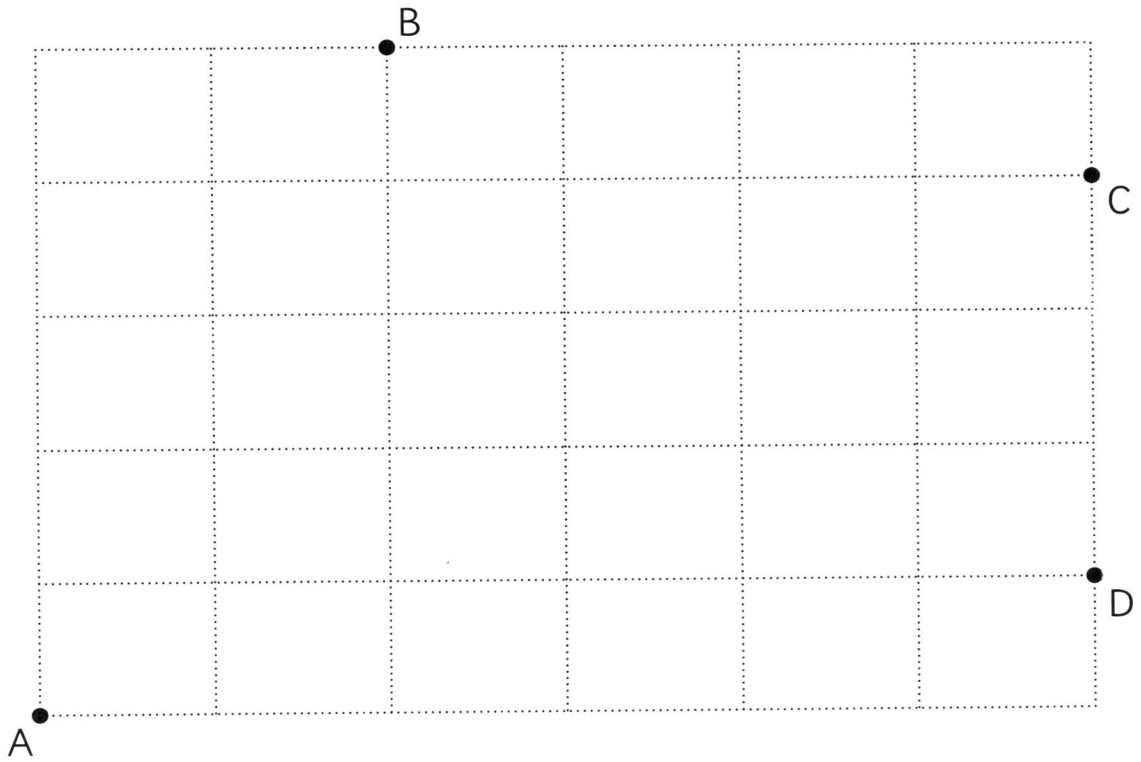

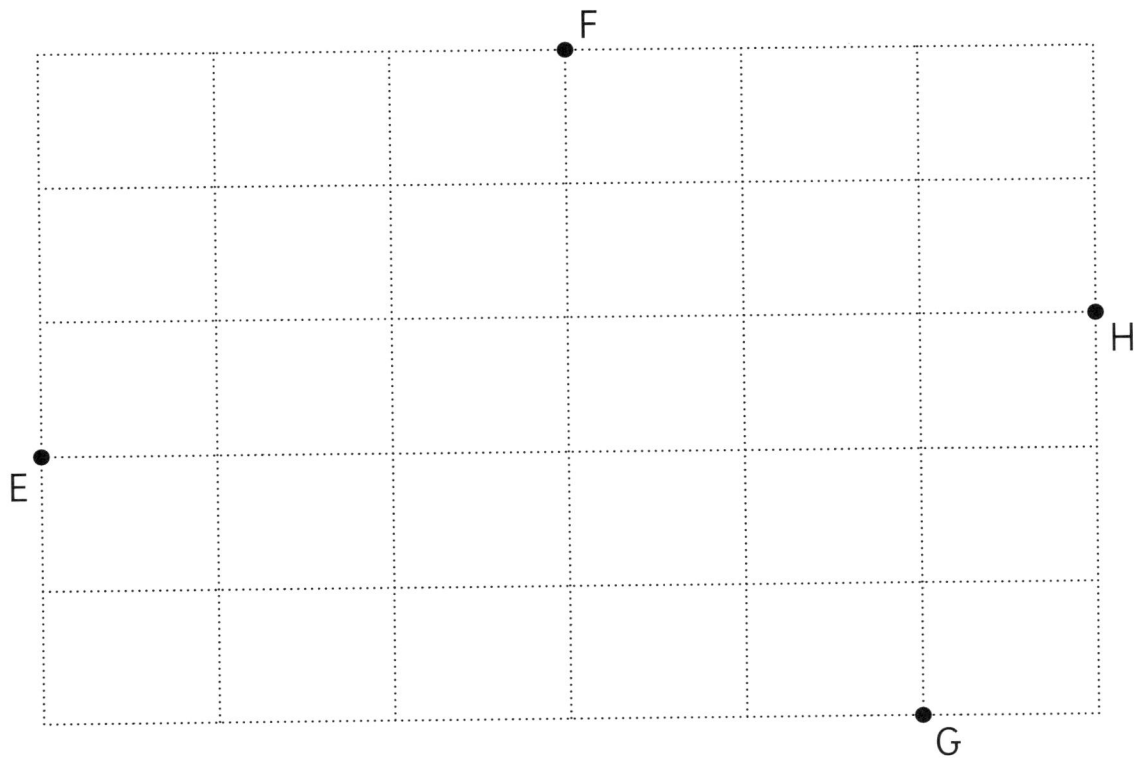

B

C

D

A

F

H

E

G

Reinforcement and Assessment

Topic Tests

Quick Maths

Key Stage 1 Practice Tests

Name _____

Date _____

Write in words:

1   7   _____

2   4   _____

3   10   _____

4   2   _____

Write in numbers:

5   nine   ☐

6   three   ☐

7   six   ☐

8   five   ☐

Count how many:

9   ● ● ● ● ● ●   ☐

10   ○ ○ ○ ○
        ○ ○ ○ ○   ☐

11   ● ● ● ● ● ● ● ● ●   ☐

Put in order, smallest first

12   7   3   9   _____

13   8   4   2   _____

14   1   6   2   9   _____

15   9   3   5   2   _____

Name

Date

1   5 + 3 = ☐

2   7 + 2 = ☐

3   Add 5 and 2 ☐

4   Four more than five? ☐

5   7 + ☐ = 10

6   ☐ + 4 = 10

7   Add three to six ☐

8   4 flowers. Pick 6 more. How many altogether? ☐

9   Write a sum that makes nine ☐ + ☐ = 9

10   3 cars. Add 4 more. How many altogether? ☐

11   Write a sum that makes eight ☐ + ☐ = 8

12   Two more than eight? ☐

13   5 + 5 = ☐

14   Seven dogs. Add three more. How many altogether? ☐

15   Write a sum that makes ten ☐ + ☐ = 10

1   1 less than 6? ☐

2   Take away five from nine ☐

3   One less than eight ☐

4   Subtract 3 from 10 ☐

5   Two less than seven? ☐

6   Count back 6 from 10 ☐

7   9 sweets. Eat 3. How many left? ☐

8   Take away seven from ten ☐

9 $10 - 5 =$ ☐

10   Count back four from nine ☐

11   What is the difference between 2 and 8? ☐

12 $10 - 4 =$ ☐

13   Ten birds. Two fly away. How many left? ☐

14 $9 -$ ☐ $= 2$

15 $10 -$ ☐ $= 3$

Name _____

Date _____

1   5p + 3p = [ ] p

2   What is this coin?   [ ] p

3   9p − 3p = [ ] p

4   How much is this?   [ ] p

5   Which two coins make 7p?   _____

6   8p − 5p = [ ] p

7   Buy two stickers at 5p each.

How much altogether? [ ] p

8   I have 10p. I spend 7p. How much is left? [ ] p

9   How much is this?   [ ] p

10   Which three coins make 9p?   _____

11   I have 10p. I spend 6p. How much is left? [ ] p

12   Buy two sweets at 4p each.

How much altogether? [ ] p

Name _____

Date _____

1   What day is it today? _____

2   How many days in a week? [ ]

3   What time is this? _____

4   What day comes after Monday? _____

5   What meal comes before lunch? _____

6   Is lunchtime before 2 o'clock? _____

7   Draw 3 o'clock on this clock

8   What day comes before Thursday? _____

9   What time is it? _____

10   Draw 8:00 on this clock

11   What day comes after Friday? _____

12   Which comes first, teatime or bedtime? _____

Name _____

Date _____

Draw a line to cut these shapes in half

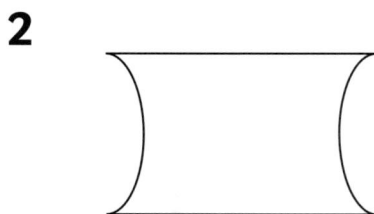

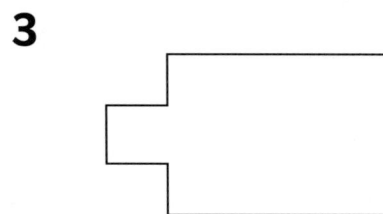

1

2

3

Have these shapes been cut in half? ✔ or ✗

4

5

6

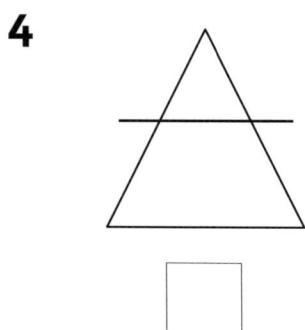

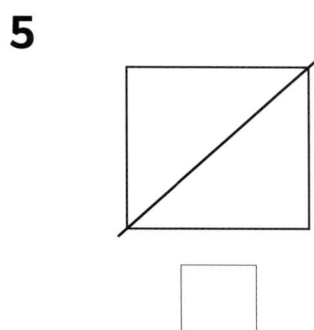

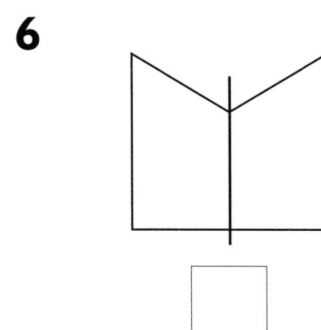

Shade half of each of these shapes

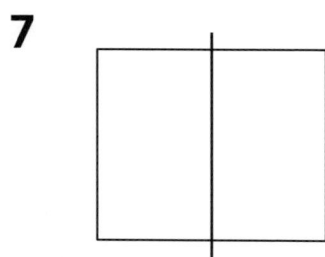

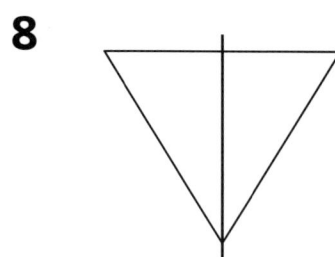

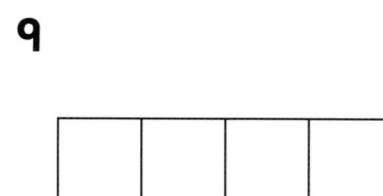

7

8

9

Name

Date

1   Is the ball above the box? _____

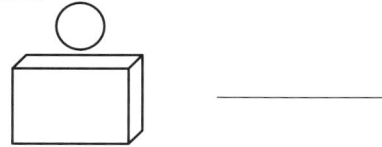

2   Is the ball beside the box? _____

3   Draw a ball on the box

4   Draw a side to finish this shape

5   How many sides has this shape?

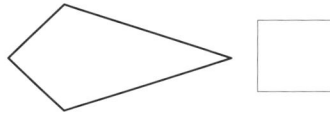

6   How many sides has this shape?

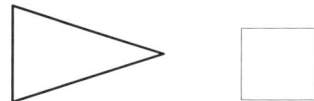

7   Put a cross on the odd one out

8   How many sides has this shape?

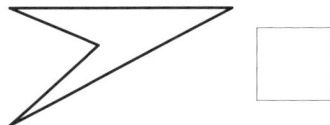

9   Are all the sides straight? _____

10 Put a cross on the odd one out

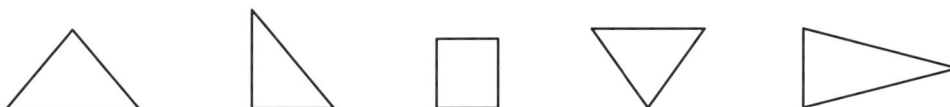

Name _____

Date _____

What comes next?

1 △ ◯ △ ◯ △ ☐

2 ◯ ◯ △ ◯ ◯ △ ◯ ☐

3 A C A B A C A B A ☐

4 1 1 2 1 1 2 1 1 2 1 1 ☐

5 M L O P M L O P M L ☐

6 3 4 1 1 3 4 1 1 3 4 1 1 3 ☐

Ring the repeating pattern

7 ◯ △ ◯ △ ◯ △

8 △ ◯ △ △ ◯ △ △ ◯ △

9 3 3 4 3 3 4 3 3 4 3 3 4

10 F H F H F H F H F H

11 4 3 2 1 4 3 2 1 4 3 2 1

Is it a repeating pattern?   ✔ or ✗

12 △ △ ◯ △ △ ◯ △ △ ◯ ☐

13 ◯ ◯ △ ◯ △ △ ◯ ◯ ◯ ☐

14 5 6 7 5 6 5 6 5 7 6 ☐

15 d c e d c d f d c e ☐

Name _____

Date _____

1   How many?   ● ● ● ● ● ● ● ●
● ● ● ● ● ● ●   [ ]

Write in words:

2   75   _____

3   91   _____

4   18   _____

Write in numbers:

5   Twelve   [ ]

6   Thirty-nine   [ ]

7   Sixty-one   [ ]

8   Write a number less than thirty but more than fifteen   [ ]

9   Write a number between fifty-three and sixty-four   [ ]

10   How many tens in 73?   [ ]

11   What is ten more than 45?   [ ]

12   What is ten less than 81?   [ ]

13   Round off 23 to the nearest ten   [ ]

14   Round off 66 to the nearest ten   [ ]

15   Put these numbers in order, smallest first

54   86   13   49   68   _____

1   14 + 3 = ☐

2   5 + 13 = ☐

3   Six more than twelve? ☐

4   Eight plus nine? ☐

5   13 + 6 = ☐

6   Add five to fourteen ☐

7   Seven biscuits. Add five more. How many altogether? ☐

8   6 + ☐ = 15

9   ☐ + 14 = 19

10   Write a sum that makes 20   ☐ + ☐ = 20

11   Nine more than eight? ☐

12   7 + 8 = ☐

13   Write a sum that makes 19   ☐ + ☐ = 19

14   9 + 9 = ☐

15   What is seven plus six? ☐

Name _____

Date _____

1 14 − 7 = ▢

2 Take seven away from twenty ▢

3 Len had twenty stamps. He used nine. How many did he

have left? ▢

4 Subtract 12 from 19 ▢

5 18 − ▢ = 9

6 20 − 6 = ▢

7 Thirteen minus eight ▢

8 ▢ − 4 = 14

9 There were twenty questions in a test. Mandy got four

wrong. How many did she get right? ▢

10 15 − 8 = ▢

11 What is the difference between 16 and 9? ▢

12 20 − ▢ = 8

13 Andy had 17 stickers. Eric had 9. How many more than Eric

did Andy have? ▢

14 16 − 8 = ▢

15 In a board game, Rachel's counter was on 18 and had to

move back 6. Where did it land? ▢

Name _____

Date _____

1   How much is this?      [   ] p

2   14p + 6p = [p   ]

3   20p − 7p = [p   ]

4   How much must I pay altogether for a sweet at 5p and a chew at 12p?   [p   ]

5   How much do two 5p coins and two 2p coins make?   [p   ]

6   Add together 7p, 3p, and 6p   [p   ]

7   Take 7p away from 14p   [p   ]

8   I have 20p and I spend 9p. How much is left?   [p]

9   Which three coins make 17p? _____

10   How much change from 20p when you spend 17p?   [p]

11   How much altogether? Three 5p coins, a 2p coin and three 1p coins?   [p   ]

12   How much change from 20p when you spend 8p?   [p]

13   Add 7p to 8p   [p   ]

14   13p less than 20p   [p   ]

Name _____

Date _____

1 What time is this?  _____

2 How many minutes in half an hour? ⬜

3 What time is one hour after 2:30? _____

4 What time is this?  _____

5 What month comes after March? _____

6 How many months in a year? ⬜

7 Make this clock show quarter past six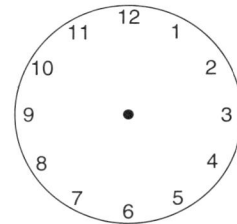

8 How many minutes in quarter of an hour? ⬜

9 What time is this?  _____

10 It is quarter to five. Draw what the time will be fifteen minutes later.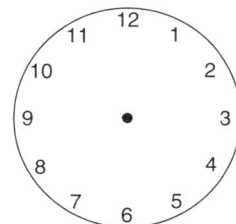

117

Name _____

Date _____

1 What fraction is shaded?

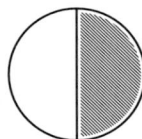

2 Shade half

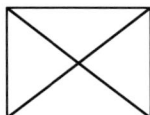

3 Colour half of the set of circles

4 What is half of 10?

5 What is quarter of 16?

6 Shade a quarter

7 What is $\frac{1}{2}$ of 14?

8 What is $\frac{1}{4}$ of 20?

9 What fraction is shaded?

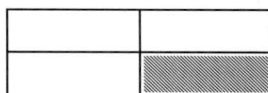

10 If half of a number is 3, what is the number?

11 If quarter of a number is 2, what is the number?

12 Harry gives half of his sweets to Nicola. She gets eight.

How many did Harry have at first?

13 What is $\frac{1}{2}$ of 18?

14 Megan cuts a ribbon into quarters. One piece is 3 cm long.

How long was the whole ribbon at first? _____ cm

Name these shapes

1 ☐   **2** ◯   **3** △

_____   _____   _____

4 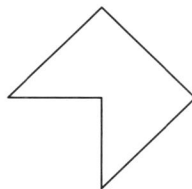   **5**   **6**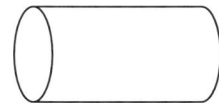

_____   _____   _____

7   Is this a hexagon?   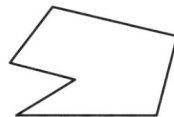   _____

8   Tick the right angles

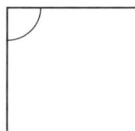      

9   What do these shapes have in common?

☐   ◇   △   ▱

_____

10   Draw another shape which
could go with the shapes above

11   If I cut a square in half I can get two triangles.

True or false?   _____

12   Is this arrow pointing left or right?   ⟵   _____

Name_____

Date_____

1   Is 7 an odd number?   _____

2   Is 13 an even number?   _____

3   What is the next number?   1, 3, 5, 7, ☐

4   Is 21 an even number?   _____

5   What is the next number?   2, 5, 8, 11, 14, ☐

6   Ring the odd numbers   12   15   8   3

7   Start on 3 and keep adding 5. Write the next two
        numbers   ☐ ☐

8   Ring the even numbers   16   19   22   13

9   What is the next number?   22, 19, 16, 13, ☐

10 Start on 2 and keep adding 3. Write the next three
        numbers   ☐ ☐ ☐

11 List the odd numbers between 22 and 30 _____

12 What is the next number?   2, 4, 6, 8, ☐

13 List the even numbers between 17 and 25 _____

14 Start on 16 and keep adding 10. Write the next three
        numbers   ☐ ☐ ☐

15 What is the next number?   2, 7, 12, 17, ☐

Name

Date   Date

Set A

1 $4 + 1 =$

2 $7 + 1 =$

3 $3 + 1 =$

4 $5 + 1 =$

5 $8 + 1 =$

6 $6 + 1 =$

7 $2 + 1 =$

8 $9 + 1 =$

9 $4 + 2 =$

10 $6 + 2 =$

11 $3 + 2 =$

12 $5 + 2 =$

13 $8 + 2 =$

14 $2 + 2 =$

15 $7 + 2 =$

Set B

1 $1 + 6 =$

2 $1 + 4 =$

3 $1 + 2 =$

4 $1 + 9 =$

5 $1 + 3 =$

6 $1 + 8 =$

7 $1 + 5 =$

8 $1 + 7 =$

9 $2 + 3 =$

10 $2 + 5 =$

11 $2 + 2 =$

12 $2 + 7 =$

13 $2 + 4 =$

14 $2 + 6 =$

15 $2 + 8 =$

Name_____

Date_____

Date_____

Set A

1 10 – 1 = ☐

2 8 – 1 = ☐

3 5 – 1 = ☐

4 7 – 1 = ☐

5 9 – 1 = ☐

6 4 – 1 = ☐

7 6 – 1 = ☐

8 3 – 1 = ☐

9 8 – 2 = ☐

10 4 – 2 = ☐

11 7 – 2 = ☐

12 5 – 2 = ☐

13 10 – 2 = ☐

14 6 – 2 = ☐

15 9 – 2 = ☐

Set B

1 5 – 3 = ☐

2 7 – 3 = ☐

3 4 – 3 = ☐

4 10 – 3 = ☐

5 8 – 3 = ☐

6 6 – 3 = ☐

7 9 – 3 = ☐

8 10 – 5 = ☐

9 10 – 7 = ☐

10 10 – 6 = ☐

11 10 – 8 = ☐

12 10 – 4 = ☐

13 10 – 9 = ☐

14 8 – 4 = ☐

15 6 – 4 = ☐

Name _____

Date _____   Date _____

Set A

1	16 + 3 =
2	14 + 2 =
3	12 + 3 =
4	17 + 2 =
5	15 + 3 =
6	16 + 2 =
7	13 + 3 =
8	11 + 2 =
9	17 + 3 =
10	18 + 2 =
11	15 + 2 =
12	14 + 3 =
13	13 + 2 =
14	11 + 3 =
15	12 + 2 =

Set B

1	4 + 10 =
2	7 + 10 =
3	6 + 9 =
4	8 + 9 =
5	3 + 10 =
6	8 + 10 =
7	5 + 9 =
8	3 + 9 =
9	2 + 10 =
10	5 + 10 =
11	7 + 9 =
12	2 + 9 =
13	6 + 10 =
14	10 + 10 =
15	9 + 9 =

Name_____

Date_____

Date_____

Set A

1 15 – 2 = ☐

2 18 – 2 = ☐

3 13 – 2 = ☐

4 16 – 2 = ☐

5 19 – 2 = ☐

6 17 – 2 = ☐

7 14 – 2 = ☐

8 12 – 2 = ☐

9 20 – 2 = ☐

10 18 – 3 = ☐

11 14 – 3 = ☐

12 20 – 3 = ☐

13 17 – 3 = ☐

14 15 – 3 = ☐

15 19 – 3 = ☐

Set B

1 17 – 10 = ☐

2 14 – 9 = ☐

3 19 – 10 = ☐

4 15 – 9 = ☐

5 13 – 10 = ☐

6 17 – 9 = ☐

7 16 – 10 = ☐

8 13 – 9 = ☐

9 18 – 10 = ☐

10 19 – 9 = ☐

11 14 – 10 = ☐

12 16 – 9 = ☐

13 20 – 10 = ☐

14 18 – 9 = ☐

15 15 – 10 = ☐

For the first group of questions you will have 5 seconds to work out the answer and write it down.

1   7 add 3.
2   9 take away 4.
3   What day is it today?
4   Write the number 7 in words.
5   6 add 2.
6   10 take away 3.
7   What is the next number in this pattern?   1, 2, 1, 2, 1, 2, 1

For the next group of questions you will have 10 seconds to work out the answer and write it down.

8   There were 5 cakes and I bought 4 more. How many cakes are there now?
9   Look at your sheet. How many sides has the shape?
10   Look at your sheet. How many dots are there?
11   What day comes after Tuesday?
12   What is 3p more than 6p?
13   What is the difference between 10 and 4?
14   Look at the numbers on your sheet. Ring the ones less than 6.
15   Is this a repeating pattern?   1 2 3 2 1 2 3 2 1 2 3 2

For the next group of questions you will have 15 seconds to work out the answer and write it down.

16   How much do a 5p coin and three 1p coins make?
17   What time does the clock on your sheet show?
18   Look at the shape on your sheet. How many straight sides has it?
19   Look at the numbers on your sheet. Put them in order, smallest first.
20   I buy a sticker for 3p and a chew for 2p. How much change do I get from 10p?

Name

Date

Total marks

Time: 5 seconds

1

2

3

4

5

6

7

Time: 10 seconds

8 cakes

9

10

11

12 p

13

14 9 4 7 3

15

Time: 15 seconds

16 p

17

18

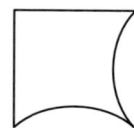

19 9 3 7

20 p

126

For the first group of questions you will have 5 seconds to work out the answer and write it down.

1   8 add 2.
2   10 take away 4.
3   What day is it today?
4   Write the number 5 in words.
5   5 add 4.
6   Subtract 5 from 8.
7   What is the next letter in this pattern?   A, L, C, A, L, C, A

For the next group of questions you will have 10 seconds to work out the answer and write it down.

8   There were 10 flowers in a pot. 5 were picked. How many were left?
9   Jack collected 6 stickers. Then he collected 4 more. How many altogether?
10   Write a sum that makes 9.
11   What day comes before Sunday?
12   I have 10p and spend 7p, how much have I left?
13   Look at the numbers on your sheet. Ring two that add to make 10.
14   Look at the numbers on your sheet. Ring two numbers with a difference of 3.
15   Look at your sheet. Draw a ball above the box.

For the next group of questions you will have 15 seconds to work out the answer and write it down.

16   Which two coins could be used to make 7p?
17   Make the clock on your sheet show 9 o'clock.
18   Look at the shape on your sheet. How many sides has it?
19   I have two 2p coins and a 5p coin. How much is that?
20   I buy two Chox for 4p each. How much change do I get from 10p?

Name_____

Date_____

Total marks [ ]

Time: 5 seconds

1 [ ]

2 [ ]

3 [   ]

4 [   ]

5 [ ]

6 [ ]

7 [ ]

Time: 10 seconds

8 [flowers]

9 [stickers]

10 [ ] + [ ] = 9

11 [   ]

12 [p]

13 [8   6   3   2]

14 [9   7   4   3]

15

Time: 15 seconds

16 [   ]

17

18

19 [p]

20 [p]

128

For the first group of questions you will have 5 seconds to work out the answer and write it down.

1   13 add 6.
2   20 take away 7.
3   How many sides has a square?
4   Write the number 12 in words.
5   9 + 9.
6   Subtract 7 from 16.
7   Look at the arrow on your sheet. Is it pointing left or right?

For the next group of questions you will have 10 seconds to work out the answer and write it down.

8   How many tens are there in 73?
9   Look at your sheet. What is the shape called?
10   Write a sum that makes 19.
11   What month comes before October?
12   I have a 10p coin and three 2p coins, how much is that?
13   Look at the numbers on your sheet. Ring two that add to make 20.
14   Round off 54 to the nearest 10.
15   What is half of 18?

For the next group of questions you will have 15 seconds to work out the answer and write it down.

16   Which three coins could be used to make 26p?
17   How long is it from half past ten to half past twelve?
18   How many faces has a cube?
19   Look at the numbers on your sheet. Ring the even numbers.
20   I have 20p and I spend 13p pence. How much have I left?

Total marks [ ]

Time: 5 seconds

1 [ ]

2 [ ]

3 [ ]

4 [   ]

5 [ ]

6 [ ]

7 [| →]

Time: 10 seconds

8 [tens]

9 [   ]

10 [ ] + [ ] = 19

11 [   ]

12 [p   ]

13 [14   3   12   6   13]

14 [ ]

15 [ ]

Time: 15 seconds

16 [   ]

17 [   ]

18 [   ]

19 [32   27   58   61]

20 [p   ]

For the first group of questions you will have 5 seconds to work out the answer and write it down.

1   What is 6 more than 7?
2   Subtract 9 from 17.
3   Is 34 an even number?
4   Write the number 62 in words.
5   8 + 7.
6   What is the difference between 16 and 8?
7   What is 20p take away 5p?

For the next group of questions you will have 10 seconds to work out the answer and write it down.

8   What is 10 less than 76?
9   What is the shape on your sheet?
10   Look at the clock on your sheet. Write it as digital time.
11   What is the third month?
12   I have a 20p coin and three 5p coins, how much is that?
13   Look at the angle on your sheet. Is it a right angle?
14   How many minutes are there in half an hour?
15   Look at the numbers on your sheet. Ring the smallest one.

For the next group of questions you will have 15 seconds to work out the answer and write it down.

16   Look at the sequence of numbers on your sheet. What number comes next?
17   What is the time three quarters of an hour after half past two?
18   Quarter of a number is 4. What is the number?
19   Look at the numbers on your sheet. Ring the odd numbers.
20   I have 20p and I buy two stamps for 9p each. How much have I left?

Name _____

Date _____

Total marks [ ]

Time: 5 seconds

1 [ ]

2 [ ]

3 [ ]

4 [   ]

5 [ ]

6 [ ]

7 [p   ]

Time: 10 seconds

8 [ ]

9 [   ]

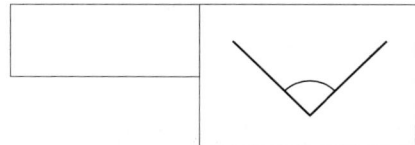

10 [   ]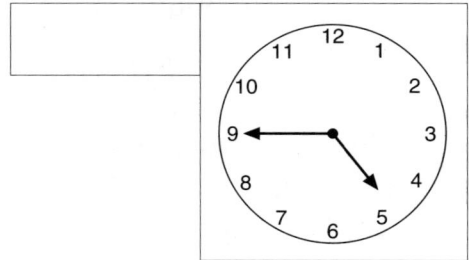

11 [   ]

12 [p   ]

13 [   ] [∨]

14 [min   ]

15 [71   17   92   29]

Time: 15 seconds

16 [1, 4, 7, 10, [ ]]

17 [   ]

18 [   ]

19 [24   31   52   47]

20 [p   ]

Answers

C1 Place value
Three
Seven
One
Ten
Six
Eight
Nine
Five
Two
Four

C2 Place value
Set A 4
Set B 3
Set C 5
Set D 2
Set E 3
Set F 5
Set G 1
Set H 4

C3 Place value
Set A 6
Set B 9
Set C 7
Set D 8
Set E 10
Set F 9
Set G 5
Set H 10

C4 Place value
Colour circles

C5 Place value
1 9
2 3
3 8
4 6
5 10
6 6
7 8
8 6
9 9

10 10
11 5
12 8
13 10
14 9

C6 Place value
1 Seventy-two
2 Fifty-eight
3 Thirty-five
4 Forty
5 Eighty-nine
6 One hundred
7 Sixty-one
8 Twenty-seven
9 Ninety-three
10 Forty-six

C7 Place value
Set A 13
Set B 17
Set C 16
Set D 20
Set E 18
Set F 14
Set G 19
Set H 15

C8 Place value
Game board

C9 Place value
1 20, 21, 23, 25
2 39, 40, 41, 43, 44
3 68, 69, 70, 71, 73
4 88, 90, 91, 92, 94, 95
5 46, 49, 50, 51, 53
6 78, 79, 80, 83, 85
7 69, 71, 74, 75, 76
8 86, 87, 88, 89, 90, 93

C10 Place value
1 17, 21, 27, 30

2 24, 36, 40, 41
3 11, 19, 20, 23
4 13, 16, 21, 31
5 27, 30, 37, 47
6 35, 49, 50, 53
7 61, 69, 70, 71
8 35, 41, 56, 68
9 19, 89, 90, 99
10 68, 79, 86, 97

C11 Place value
1 7, 3
2 9, 5
3 6, 2
4 5, 4
5 3, 8
6 8, 6
7 4, 7
8 2, 1
9 9, 9
10 8, 0

C12 Place value
1 42, 52
2 49, 69, 79
3 14, 44, 54
4 45, 35
5 73, 63, 43
6 15, 45, 55
7 17, 27, 57, 67
8 60, 80, 90, 100
9 78, 68, 48, 38
10 41, 31, 11, 1

C13 Place value
1 10
2 10
3 30
4 50
5 50
6 70
7 90
8 60
9 80
10 40

C14 Addition
1 5
2 4
3 4
4 3
5 5
6 5
7 5
8 3
9 3
10 5
11 4
12 4
Own sums to make 4 and 5

C15 Addition
1 6, 7
2 5, 6
3 9, 10
4 4, 5
5 7, 8
6 3, 4
7 8, 9
8 6, 7
9 4, 5
10 9, 10

C16 Addition
Set A 6, 8
Set B 5, 7
Set C 8, 10
Set D 4, 6
Set E 3, 5
Set F 7, 9
Set G 5, 7
Set H 8, 10

C17 Addition
Set A 3, 6
Set B 5, 8
Set C 6, 9
Set D 4, 7
Set E 2, 5
Set F 7, 10

Set G 3, 7
Set H 6, 10
Set I 4, 8

C18 Addition
1 8
2 7
3 8
4 8
5 10
6 9
7 10
8 10
9 9
10 9
11 9
12 10
Own sums to make 10

C19 Addition
1 $5 + 3 = 8$
2 $6 + 2 = 8$
3 $4 + 3 = 7$
4 $8 + 2 = 10$
5 $3 + 6 = 9$
6 $5 + 4 = 9$
7 $4 + 6 = 10$
8 $7 + 3 = 10$
9 $2 + 7 = 9$
10 $5 + 5 = 10$

C20 Addition
Ring the sums:
$4 + 6$
$3 + 7$
$9 + 1$
$1 + 9$
$7 + 3$
$5 + 5$
$8 + 2$
$2 + 8$
$10 + 0$

C21 Addition
1 11, 9, 11
2 11, 11, 9
3 9, 11, 9
4 9, 11, 11
5 9, 11, 11
6 11, 9, 11

C22 Addition
1 12, 11, 13
2 8, 7, 9
3 18, 19, 17
4 6, 7, 7
5 14, 13, 15
6 10, 9, 11
7 18, 17, 19
8 16, 15, 17

9 12, 13, 11
10 14, 15, 13

C23 Addition
Variety of answers possible

C24 Addition
1 Fifteen
2 Eighteen
3 Fifteen
4 Fourteen
5 Thirteen
6 Twenty
7 Nineteen
8 Nineteen
9 Seventeen
10 Twenty

C25 Addition
Own sums to make 18 and 19

C26 Addition
11 = {10 + 1, 1 + 10, 2 + 9}
12 = {2 + 10, 9 + 3, 3 + 9}
13 = {3 + 10, 4 + 9}
14 = {10 + 4, 4 + 10, 9 + 5, 5 + 9}
15 = {5 + 10, 10 + 5, 6 + 9, 9 + 6}
16 = {6 + 10, 10 + 6, 7 + 9, 9 + 7}
17 = {10 + 7, 7 + 10, 8 + 9, 9 + 8}
18 = {8 + 10, 10 + 8, 9 + 9}
19 = {9 + 10, 10 + 9, 9 + 10, 10 + 9}
20 = {10 + 10}

C27 Addition
1 13
2 20
3 16
4 18
5 13
6 14
7 19
8 17
9 18
10 20

C28 Addition
1 3
2 4, 2
3 7, 5, 4
4 5, 4, 2
5 4, 1, 0

6 8, 6, 5
7 6, 5, 3
8 9, 6, 5

C29 Addition
Ring the sums:
$4 - 2$
$3 - 1$
$5 - 3$
Ring the sums:
$3 - 0$
$4 - 1$
$5 - 2$

C30 Subtraction
1 4, 3
2 10, 9
3 3, 2
4 6, 5
5 8, 7
6 5, 4
7 10, 9
8 9, 8
9 7, 6
10 5, 4

C31 Subtraction
1 3
2 2
3 5
4 4
5 5
6 5
7 5
8 6

C32 Subtraction
Set A 6, 3
Set B 9, 6
Set C 7, 4
Set D 5, 2
Set E 10, 7
Set F 8, 5
Set G 8, 4
Set H 10, 6
Set I 9, 5

C33 Subtraction
Set A $7 - 2$
Set B $9 - 4$
Set C $6 - 1$
Set D $8 - 3$
Set E $10 - 5$
Set F $7 - 2$
Set G $10 - 4$
Set H $10 - 7$
Set I $10 - 6$
Set J $10 - 3$

C34 Subtraction
Set A 1 2

2 4
3 1
4 3
Set B 1 5
2 3
3 2
4 4
Set C 1 6
2 3
3 5
4 4
5 2
Set D 1 6
2 4
3 2
4 5
5 3
Set E 1 6
2 3
3 8
4 5
5 4
6 7

C35 Subtraction
1 ✔
2 ✔
3 ✘ Four
4 ✔
5 ✔
6 ✔
7 ✘ Six
8 ✔
9 ✘ Three
10 ✔

C36 Subtraction
1 8, 7
2 6, 7
3 9, 10
4 10, 11
5 7, 6
6 8, 9
7 6, 5
8 7, 8
9 8, 9
10 7, 8

C37 Subtraction
Own sums

C38 Subtraction
Difference of 7:
15, 8
14, 7
12, 5
6, 13
11, 4

Difference of 8:
19, 11

6, 14
15, 7
17, 9
16, 8
11, 3
4, 12

C39 Subtraction
1 $12 - 8 = 4$
2 $14 - 5 = 9$
3 $18 - 9 = 9$
4 $16 - 7 = 9$
5 $17 - 9 = 8$
6 $20 - 14 = 6$
7 $19 - 12 = 7$
8 $18 - 11 = 7$
9 $15 - 7 = 8$
10 $20 - 12 = 8$

C40 Money
1p coins coloured;
2p coins ringed

C41 Money
5p coins coloured;
10p coins crossed

C42 Money
Coins coloured
that make up 5p, 4p
and 6p

C43 Money
Coins drawn to make
specified amounts.

Variety of answers
possible

C44 Money
To make 10p,
rings around:
4p + 6p
7p + 3p
9p + 1p
6p + 4p
8p + 2p
5p + 5p

To make 9p,
rings around:
5p+ 4p
2p + 7p
3p + 6p

C45 Money
1 1p
2 3p
3 2p

1 8p

2 5p
3 3p
4 0p
5 9p
6 2p
7 4p
8 6p
9 1p
10 7p

C46 Money
1 $2p + 3p = 5p$
2 $3p + 3p = 6p$
3 $4p + 2p = 6p$
4 $5p + 4p = 9p$
5 $2p + 5p = 7p$
6 $5p + 5p = 10p$
7 $2p + 3p + 4p = 9p$

C47 Money
1 4p, 6p
2 7p, 3p
3 8p, 2p
4 7p, 3p
5 8p, 2p
6 8p, 2p
7 9p, 1p

C48 Money
1 5p, 4p
2 10p, 3p
3 10p, 7p
4 20p, 5p
5 20p, 1p
6 10p, 9p
7 20p, 14p
8 20p, 7p
9 10p, 5p
10 20p, 11p

C49 Money
Set A 2p
Set B 1p
Set C 2p
Set D 2p
Set E 5p
Set F 5p
Set G 5p
Set H 10p

C50 Money
Set A 1 12p
2 15p
3 20p
4 13p
5 19p
Set B 1 9p
2 15p
3 20p
4 14p
5 12p

Set C 1 15p
2 19p
3 14p
4 20p
5 17p
Set D 1 17p
2 15p
3 19p
4 12p
5 18p

C51 Money
1 5p
2 6p
3 4p
4 3p
5 7p
6 8p
7 8p
8 5p
9 6p
10 9p
11 6p
12 8p
13 6p
14 8p
15 12p
16 8p
17 11p
18 9p
19 9p
20 9p

C52 Money
1 ✔
2 ✗
3 ✔
4 ✗
5 ✔
6 ✔
7 ✗
8 ✔
9 ✗
10 ✗
11 ✔
12 ✔
13 ✔
14 ✗
15 ✗
16 ✗
17 ✔
18 ✗
19 ✔
20 ✔

C53 Money
1 4p
2 1p
3 2p
4 3p

1 15p
2 6p
3 10p
4 2p
5 11p
6 5p
7 7p
8 12p
9 8p
10 4p
11 13p
12 9p

C54 Money
1 7p
2 10p, 5p, 1p
3 15p
4 18p
5 20p
6 10p, 2p, 1p
7 11p
8 17p

C55 Time
1 Tuesday
2 Friday
3 Wednesday
4 Saturday
5 Wednesday
6 Tuesday
7 Saturday
8 Thursday
9 Sunday
10 Friday

C56 Time
1 4 o'clock
2 1 o'clock
3 7 o'clock
4 9 o'clock
5 8 o'clock
6 3 o'clock
7 *Clock to show*
2 o'clock

8 *Clock to show*
10 o'clock

9 *Clock to show
6 o'clock*

10 *Clock to show
11 o'clock*

C57 Time
1 3:00
2 7:00
3 *Clock to show
10 o'clock*

4 4:00
5 *Clock to show
5 o'clock*

6 *Clock to show
8 o'clock*

7 2:00
8 *Clock to show
6 o'clock*

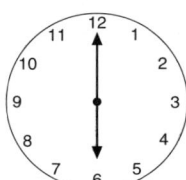

C58 Time
1 Sunday,
Wednesday
2 Wednesday,
Saturday
3 Saturday,
Tuesday
4 Thursday,
Sunday
5 Tuesday,
Thursday
6 Saturday,
Friday
7 Wednesday,
Friday
8 Monday,
Sunday
9 Friday,
Sunday

C59 Time
*Months joined
in order*

1 April
2 September
3 December
4 June
5 November
6 February

C60 Time
1 Quarter past six
2 Half past ten
3 Quarter to five
4 Seven o'clock
5 Quarter past
three
6 Quarter to three
7 Half past three
8 Nine o'clock
9 Half past eleven
10 Quarter to four
11 Quarter past one
12 Quarter to eight

C61 Time
Clocks to show:

1

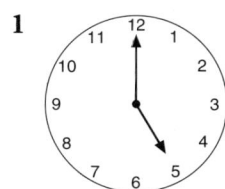

2 7:30

3 2:15

4 9:30

5 6:15

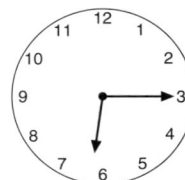

6 7:45

7 2:45

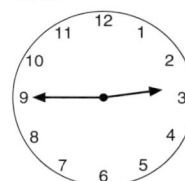

C62 Time
Join:
1 hour to 60 minutes
2 hours to 120 minutes
15 minutes to $\frac{1}{4}$ hour
30 minutes to $\frac{1}{2}$ hour
$\frac{3}{4}$ hour to 45 minutes

1 60
2 30
3 15
4 2
5 $\frac{3}{4}$
6 $\frac{1}{2}$

C63 Time
1 1 hour
2 1 hour
3 1 hour
4 2 hours
5 $\frac{1}{2}$ hour

6 $\frac{1}{2}$ hour
7 $\frac{1}{4}$ hour
8 $\frac{3}{4}$ hour
9 $\frac{3}{4}$ hour
10 $\frac{1}{2}$ hour

C64 Time
Clocks to show:

1 3:15

2 4:45

3 10:45

4 1:45

5 8:00

6 1:00

136

7 11:15

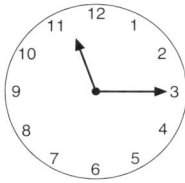

8 4:45

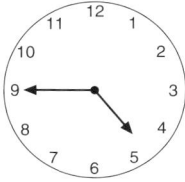

C65 Fractions
One line drawn to make halves.
Possible lines shown.

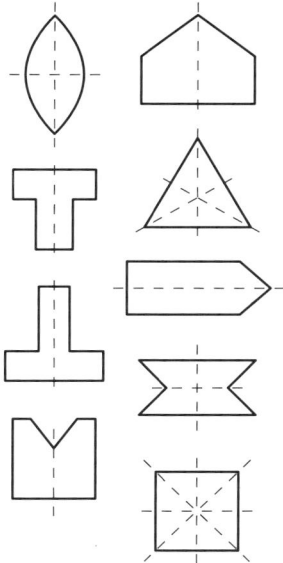

C66 Fractions
Missing half drawn

C67 Fractions
One section shaded

C68 Fractions
Boxes should show:
- **1** 6, 6, 3
- **2** 4, 4, 2
- **3** 12, 12, 6
- **4** 10, 10, 5
- **5** 18, 18, 9
- **6** 14, 14, 7
- **7** 16, 16, 8
- **8** 20, 20, 10

C69 Fractions
- **1** 5
- **2** 2
- **3** 2
- **4** 7
- **5** 1

- **6** 3
- **7** 9
- **8** 6
- **9** 4
- **10** 10
- **11** 8
- **12** 3
- **13** 1
- **14** 5

- **1** 12
- **2** 6
- **3** 11
- **4** 13

C70 Fractions
- **1** ✔
- **2** ✘
- **3** ✘
- **4** ✔
- **5** ✔
- **6** ✔
- **7** ✔
- **8** ✘
- **9** ✔
- **10** ✘

- **1** ✘
- **2** ✘
- **3** ✔
- **4** ✔
- **5** ✘
- **6** ✔
- **7** ✔
- **8** ✔
- **9** ✘
- **10** ✘

C71 Fractions
Set A
- **1** 8
- **2** 8
- **3** 16
- **4** 12
- **5** 12
- **6** 2
- **7** 16
- **8** 22

Set B
- **1** 18
- **2** 20
- **3** 20
- **4** 6
- **5** 4
- **6** 10
- **7** 14
- **8** 24

C72 Pattern
1 △

---

2 □

3 □

4 □

5 △

6 □

7 ○ □

8 △ △

C73 Pattern
1 *Done*

2
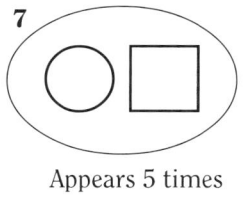
Appears 3 times

3
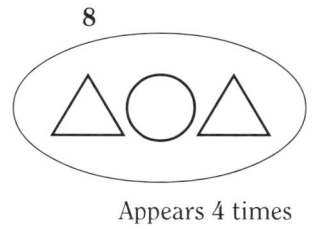
Appears 5 times

4
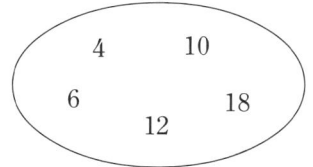
Appears 3 times

5
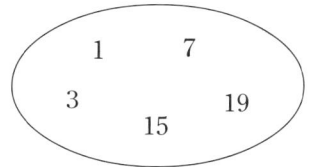
Appears twice

6
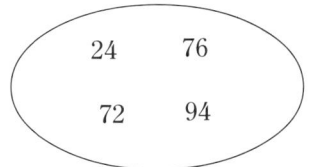
Appears 3 times

7
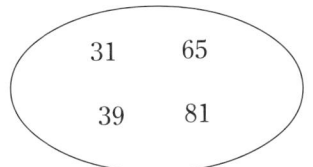
Appears 5 times

8

Appears 4 times

C74 Pattern
A *Even numbers:*
4, 6, 10, 12, 18

4   10
6   18
  12

Odd numbers:
1, 3, 7, 15, 19

1   7
3   19
  15

B *Even numbers:*
24, 72, 76, 94

24   76
72   94

Odd numbers:
31, 39, 65, 81

31   65
39   81

C
- **1** 15
- **2** 14
- **3** 23

C75 Pattern
- **1** 12, 14
- **2** 15, 18
- **3** 15, 19
- **4** 32, 34

5	27, 29
6	4, 2
7	16, 19
8	3, 1
9	11, 17
10	37, 41

C76 Pattern

1	7, 10, 13
2	11, 13, 15
3	14, 17, 20
4	10, 15, 25
5	14, 16, 18, 20
6	18, 23, 28, 33
7	24, 34, 44
8	15, 18, 21, 24
9	36, 46, 56, 66
10	26, 31, 36, 41

C77 Pattern

1	16, 14, 12
2	40, 30, 20, 10
3	27, 24, 21, 18
4	25, 20, 15, 10
5	62, 52, 42, 32
6	37, 35, 33, 31
7	43, 40, 37, 34
8	51, 41, 31, 21
9	37, 32, 27, 22
10	77, 67, 57, 47

C78 Shape and Space

Three sides: a, d, f

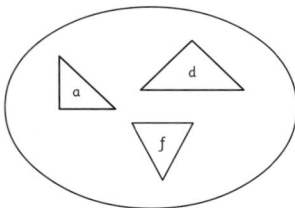

Four sides: b, c, e, g

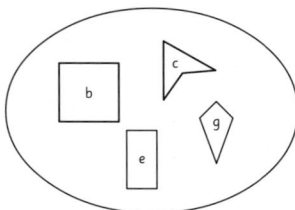

All straight sides:
b, d, f

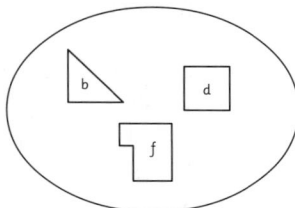

Not all straight sides:
a, c, e, g

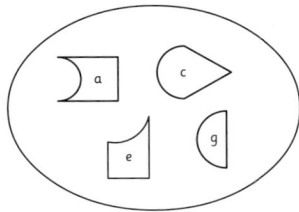

C79 Shape and Space

Four sides: e, f

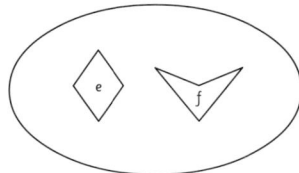

Five sides: a, b, g

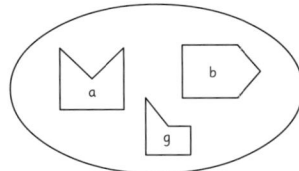

Six sides: c, d

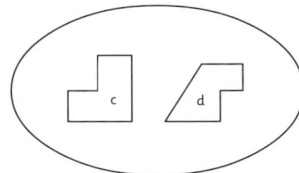

1	Pentagon
2	Circle
3	Hexagon
4	Rectangle
5	Pentagon
6	Triangle

C80 Shape and Space

1	Cuboid
2	Sphere
3	Pyramid
4	Cone
5	Cuboid
6	Cylinder
7	Cuboid
8	Cylinder
9	Cube

C81 Shape and Space

*Answers depend on
instructions given*

C82 Topic Tests

1	Seven
2	Four
3	Ten
4	Two
5	9
6	3

7	6
8	5
9	6
10	8
11	9
12	3, 7, 9
13	2, 4, 8
14	1, 2, 6, 9
15	2, 3, 5, 9

C83 Topic Tests

1	8
2	9
3	7
4	9
5	3
6	6
7	9
8	10
9	*Own sum to make 9*
10	7
11	*Own sum to make 8*
12	10
13	10
14	10
15	*Own sum to make 10*

C84 Topic Tests

1	5
2	4
3	7
4	7
5	5
6	4
7	6
8	3
9	5
10	5
11	6
12	6
13	8
14	7
15	7

C85 Topic Tests

1	8p
2	10p
3	6p
4	5p
5	5p, 2p
6	3p
7	10p
8	3p
9	8p
10	5p, 2p, 2p
11	4p
12	8p

C86 Topic Tests

1	*(Today)*
2	7
3	9 o'clock
4	Tuesday
5	Breakfast
6	Yes
7	*Clock to show 3 o'clock*

8	Wednesday
9	7 o'clock
10	*Clock to show 8 o'clock*

11	Saturday
12	Teatime

C87 Topic Tests

Line drawn to cut shapes in half

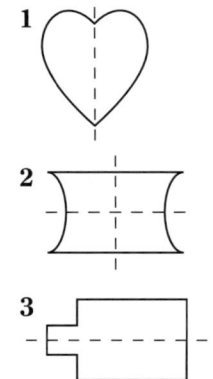

4	✗
5	✔
6	✔

Half shaded

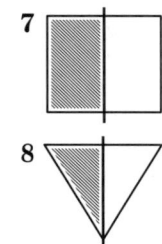

9

C88 Topic Tests
1 Yes
2 Yes
3
4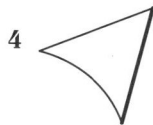
5 4
6 3
7
8 4
9 No
10

C89 Topic Tests
1
2
3 C
4 2
5 O
6 4
7
8
9
10
11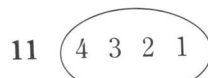
12 ✔
13 ✗
14 ✗
15 ✗

C90 Topic Tests
1 15
2 Seventy-five
3 Ninety-one
4 Eighteen
5 12
6 39
7 61
8 *Number between 15 and 30*
9 *Number between 53 and 64*
10 7
11 55
12 71
13 20
14 70
15 13, 49, 54, 68, 86

C91 Topic Tests
1 17
2 18
3 18
4 17
5 19
6 19
7 12
8 9
9 5
10 *Own sum to make 20*
11 17
12 15
13 *Own sum to make 19*
14 18
15 13

C92 Topic Tests
1 7
2 13
3 11
4 7
5 9
6 14
7 5
8 18
9 16
10 7
11 7
12 12
13 8
14 8
15 12

C93 Topic Tests
1 16p
2 20p
3 13p
4 17p
5 14p
6 16p
7 7p
8 11p
9 10p, 5p, 2p
10 3p
11 20p
12 12p
13 15p
14 7p

C94 Topic Tests
1 Half past ten
2 30
3 3:30
4 Quarter to two
5 April
6 12
7 *Clock to show quarter past six*

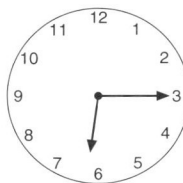

8 15
9 Quarter to eight
10 *Clock to show five o'clock*

C95 Topic Tests
1 $\frac{1}{2}$
2 Half shaded
3 Six circles coloured
4 5
5 4
6 Quarter shaded
7 7
8 5
9 $\frac{1}{4}$
10 6
11 8
12 16
13 9
14 12 cm

C96 Topic Tests
1 Square
2 Circle
3 Triangle
4 Cube
5 Pentagon
6 Cylinder
7 Yes
8 *1st and 4th angles ticked*
9 Four straight sides
10 *Own shape drawn with four straight sides*
11 True
12 Left

C97 Topic Tests
1 Yes
2 No
3 9
4 No
5 17
6 *Numbers ringed:* 15, 3
7 8, 13
8 *Numbers ringed:* 16, 22
9 10
10 5, 8, 11
11 23, 25, 27, 29
12 10
13 18, 20, 22, 24
14 26, 36, 46
15 22

C98 Quick Maths
Set A **1** 5
2 8
3 4
4 6
5 9
6 7
7 3
8 10
9 6
10 8
11 5
12 7
13 10
14 4
15 9
Set B **1** 7
2 5
3 3
4 10
5 4
6 9
7 6
8 8
9 5
10 7
11 4
12 9
13 6
14 8
15 10

C99 Quick Maths

Set A
1 9
2 7
3 4
4 6
5 8
6 3
7 5
8 2
9 6
10 2
11 5
12 3
13 8
14 4
15 7

Set B
1 2
2 4
3 1
4 7
5 5
6 3
7 6
8 5
9 3
10 4
11 2
12 6
13 1
14 4
15 2

C100 Quick Maths

Set A
1 19
2 16
3 15
4 19
5 18
6 18
7 16
8 13
9 20
10 20
11 17
12 17
13 15
14 14
15 14

Set B
1 14
2 17
3 15
4 17
5 13
6 18
7 14
8 12
9 12
10 15
11 16
12 11
13 16

14 20
15 18

C101 Quick Maths

Set A
1 13
2 16
3 11
4 14
5 17
6 15
7 12
8 10
9 18
10 15
11 11
12 17
13 14
14 12
15 16

Set B
1 7
2 5
3 9
4 6
5 3
6 8
7 6
8 4
9 8
10 10
11 4
12 7
13 10
14 9
15 5

C102 KS1 Practice Tests
Question sheet

C103 KS1 Practice Tests
1 10
2 5
3 (Today)
4 Seven
5 8
6 7
7 2
8 9
9 4
10 7
11 Wednesday
12 9p
13 6
14 *Numbers ringed:*
   3, 4
15 No
16 8p
17 4 o'clock
18 2
19 3, 7, 9
20 5p

C104 KS1 Practice Tests
Question sheet

C105 KS1 Practice Tests
1 10
2 6
3 (Today)
4 Five
5 9
6 3
7 L
8 5
9 10
10 *Own sum to make 9*
11 Saturday
12 3p
13 *Numbers ringed:*
   8, 2
14 *Numbers ringed:*
   7, 4
15

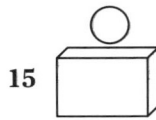

16 5p, 2p
17 *Clock to show 9 o'clock*

18 4
19 9p
20 2p

C106 KS1 Practice Tests
Question sheet

C107 KS1 Practice Tests
1 19
2 13
3 4
4 Twelve
5 18
6 9
7 Right
8 7
9 Pentagon
10 *Own sum to make 19*
11 September
12 16p
13 *Numbers ringed:*
   14, 6
14 50
15 9
16 20p, 5p, 1p
17 2 hours

18 6
19 *Numbers ringed:*
   32, 58
20 7p

C108 KS1 Practice Tests
Question sheet

C109 KS1 Practice Tests
1 13
2 8
3 Yes
4 Sixty-two
5 15
6 8
7 15p
8 66
9 Hexagon
10 4:45
11 March
12 35p
13 Yes
14 30 min
15 *Number ringed:*
   17
16 13
17 Quarter past three
18 16
19 *Numbers ringed:*
   31, 47
20 2p